Early Floral Engravings

All 110 plates from the 1612 "Florilegium" by

Emanuel Sweerts

EDITED BY E. F. BLEILER

Dover Publications, Inc., New York

ACKNOWLEDGMENTS

The New York Public Library; the Library of the
Horticultural Society of New York; the Library of the
Bronx Botanical Garden; Kew Gardens, England, for
information on de Bry; the Library of the Massachu-
setts Horticultural Society for the portrait of Sweerts,
which appears in their 1631 edition of the *Florilegium*.

Copyright © 1976 by Dover Publications, Inc.
All rights reserved under Pan American and International
Copyright Conventions.

Published in Canada by General Publishing Company, Ltd.,
30 Lesmill Road, Don Mills, Toronto, Ontario.
Published in the United Kingdom by Constable and Company, Ltd.,
3 The Lanchesters, 162–164 Fulham Palace Road, London W6 9ER.

This Dover edition, a 1991 revised version of *Early Floral Engrav-
ings*, first published in 1976, contains all the plates from *Florilegium
Emanuelis Sweerti Septimonti Batavi Amsteledami co[m]morantis, tractans de
variis florib[us] et aliis indicis pla[n]tis ad vivum delineatum in duabus partib[us] et quatuor linguis concinnatum*, published by the author, and
printed by Anthonius Kempner (first part) and Erasmus Kempffer
(second part), in Frankfurt am Main, 1612.

E. F. Bleiler has written specially for the present edition: an
introduction; translations of the original advertisement, preface
and planting instructions; identifying captions that incorporate
material from the original text (following the plates); and an index
to the plates.

DOVER *Pictorial Archive* SERIES

International Standard Book Number: 0-486-23038-4
Library of Congress Catalog Card Number: 73-76963

Manufactured in the United States of America
Dover Publications, Inc.
31 East 2nd Street
Mineola, N.Y. 11501

INTRODUCTION
TO THE DOVER EDITION

Illustrated herbals had long been important in European publishing and science, but around the beginning of the seventeenth century floral illustration took a new direction in Europe. The flower became evident as a thing of beauty in itself, not simply as a decoration for a handicraft nor as an adjunct to botany or medicine. In painting, the floral still life became important with Roelant Savery and Jan Breughel, and in book publishing, the florilegium was devised. This was a collection of flower plates, usually printed by copperplate, as opposed to the woodcut art of the older illustrations, and often without significant text. The first few florilegia were intended as design sources. Such were the twenty-four plates that Aedriaen Collaert produced sometime before 1600, and the plates of the gardener-artist Vallet, who recorded plants from the French royal gardens as sewing patterns for Marie de Medici. But by 1611 the concept of flower plates for their own sakes had been established. In this year J. T. de Bry began his series of *Icones Plantarum* (*Florilegium Novum*), moving the focal point from the botanist's collecting case to the garden.

One of the more noteworthy of these early floral books is the sumptuous *Florilegium* of Emanuel Sweerts. First printed in Frankfurt am Main in 1612, it was reissued in 1614, and then reprinted in Amsterdam in 1620, 1631, 1641, 1647 and 1655. The earlier editions carry the secondary note of being nursery catalogues; the later editions, with plates reengraved on a somewhat inferior level, no longer offer plants for sale, but are frankly floral copperplates for their own sake.

Emanuel Sweerts (Latinized Sweertius, Germanized Schwertz) maintained a dual career. Born in Zevenbergen in the Netherlands in 1552, a resident of Amsterdam for most of his adult life, he was a minor artist who occasionally did portraits and other painting. More important, however, he was the proprietor of what might be called a commercial museum, and a purveyor of novelties to the wealthy of Europe. He collected and sold to his clients stuffed birds, crystals, sea shells, mineral specimens, ethnographic novelties and floral stock. As he says in his preface, flowers were his greatest delight; even allowing for conventional rhetoric, a modern can see that Sweerts was truly moved by the beauties of the floral world.

For part of the year Sweerts operated his service from Amsterdam; at other times he held shop at the annual Frankfurt fair. He also had the honor of being purveyor to the gardens of the half-mad Habsburg Emperor in Vienna, Kaiser Rudolph II, coming into association at times with the botanist Clusius (de l'Ecluse). We do not know whether Sweerts travelled extensively otherwise. In general, however, he seems to have been a middleman, buying his wares from the ships that returned from strange seas and from the stocks of the more scientifically minded botanist-dealers. Sweerts died in the latter part of 1612, survived by his wife and children, who seem to have carried on his business for at least a couple of years.

Today, in addition to the *Florilegium* Sweerts finds a place in dictionaries of biography as the progenitor of a long series of Dutch painters and literati, extending well into the eighteenth century. Cornelis and Hieronymus Sweerts are the most important of these. Sweerts is also remembered through a white Iris, *Iris swerti*, and Linnaeus honored him by naming after him a genus of plants related to the Gentian, the *Swertia*.

We know practically nothing of Sweerts beyond these brief biographical basics. But if we are allowed to construct a personality from a nursery catalogue plus a little prefatory material, we may draw a few conclusions about Sweerts the man. He was intelligent, abreast of the botanical knowledge of his day, able to work adequately with several languages, including Latin. He was ambitious, gifted with business acumen; shrewd, perhaps somewhat tricky in the manner of the medieval merchant, but honest in other respects; perhaps not imaginative or creative; proud of his association with the great of the day; pedantically careful until the last moment, at which time he might let go in frank despair; filled with a sense of beauty of nature; possibly a little childlike and naïve. Whether or not these comments are correct, Sweerts's personality is now lost in the past, and he remains with us only in the 110 plates of his *Florilegium*.

THE PLATES

Sweerts's book seems to have been in preparation for some three years. He received the Imperial Copyright in 1609 (which copyright, in contradistinction to a modern copyright, could be issued before a book was prepared), but it was not until late 1612, at the earliest, that his book was finished. It is always possible that the book did not appear for sale before 1613. Sweerts's preface is dated September 1612, and his book still had to be typeset in part, printed and bound.

During this time, which is not unreasonably long for a book of this size and type, Sweerts presumably prepared his drawings, gathered other picture material and had it cut in copper. His publisher may have had some hand in the German text, if the cryptic comment about the pineapple on Plate II-31 is interpreted correctly. Who cut Sweerts's plates, however, whether Dutchmen or Germans, is not known, although it would seem obvious from internal evidence that at least five men worked on them. These engravers varied from quite competent to somewhat incompetent. Since there is the further matter of different engraving techniques, Sweerts's plates show considerable variety in quality and style.

A modern reader may wonder why Sweerts did not exert more control over his project, dismissing the poor workmen, insisting on greater uniformity of style, correcting the occasional mistakes in botany, and tidying the lettering. No answers are known, although we may speculate. Possibly the book was finished hastily in Germany—since de Bry's similar florilegium of 1611 was quite successful—and Sweerts was unable to supervise the plates. Or, since Sweerts was footing the bills, he may have been cutting costs by using cheap labor. A third possibility is that Sweerts was incapacitated during the time the plates were being finished. His preface has a note of death-religiosity in it, and he died a short time after he signed it. In any case, it can well be said that Sweerts's engravers did not always do him justice.

The plates in the *Florilegium* were not completely original. Many of the better bulbous plants were derived from de Bry's *Icones Plantarum*, which has already been mentioned. Sweerts adapted some of them by adding bulbs and foliage, to complete the image of the plant. De Bry, however, had taken several from Vallet's *Jardin du tres Chrestien Henry IV* (1608), which Sweerts may also have used directly. De Bry, however, returned Sweerts's compliment later, for when de Bry issued the second, third and fourth parts of his *Icones* over the next decade, he pilfered heavily from Sweerts.

Sweerts also drew on other, older books, particularly for his fibrous-rooted plants. Here he took illustrations from the general botanical chain, from Clusius for Spanish and Balkan plants, from Matthioli-Camerarius, and from L'Obel's enormous collection of traditional botanical woodcuts. Certain of Sweerts's plates, however, seem to be original, and it is presumed that Sweerts drew them himself.

A word need be said about these borrowings. They are not necessarily plagiarisms. Sixteenth and seventeenth-century botanists often shared their cuts willingly, and the general feeling was that the botanist did not have proprietary rights. This was frankly expressed by Clusius, L'Obel and their associates. There is also the peculiar legal situation surrounding Sweerts's book. Sweerts held an Imperial Copyright, which meant that no one else could use his material within the somewhat vague domain of the Holy Roman Empire—on pain of fine, destruction of books and other punishment. That de Bry could have used Sweerts's plates later implies that some understanding was probably reached between de Bry and the Sweerts family, otherwise de Bry could not have sold his book in the Empire. Such an agreement may well have included Sweerts's earlier use of de Bry's material.

Sweerts has been criticized in the literature for offering reprint art rather than original work. This criticism is based on a misunderstanding of Sweerts's Latin text. Sweerts never claimed to offer original drawings, a claim that has been put in his mouth. Sweerts offered plants drawn *ad vivum*, not *a vivo*—not ''from life'' but ''to the life.''

There is a good possibility that Sweerts never saw his book completed; nevertheless, his personality still informs it. Honesty as a dealer is the general note. It is well known that nurserymen are not on their oath when they portray their stock, and it is to Sweerts's credit that his pictures are reliable from a gardening point of view. The flowers are not exaggerated, and the descriptions are honest. Sweerts was candid enough to say when he had not seen certain plants in blossom, and he raised no false hopes on the part of the buyer. There are very few illustrations in his book that might be called deceptive, and these few can be accounted for via traditional representations.

Sweerts was not the first to illustrate plants in full size, despite his preface, but he does seem to have a primacy as a cataloguer. We know of no earlier merchant's catalogue, and it was long before another catalogue appeared that could come even close to matching Sweerts's in variety and splendor. Indeed, that Sweerts could gather together such an assortment of stock is indicative of great energy and resourcefulness.

THE PLANTS

Sweerts's plants were the children of his time. He was living in the middle of winds of horticultural expansion. The Orient, for example, was pouring ornamentals into Europe. Busbecq, Ambassador from the Holy Roman Empire to the Grande Porte, initiated a wave of Tulips, Narcissuses, Anemones, Crocuses and other spring-flowering bulbs that have dominated our gardens ever since. This occurred within Sweerts's lifetime. Waves of trade, too, enriched Europe's flower resources from the Near East. Clusius was everywhere. Clusius brought new plants from Turkey. Clusius introduced the yellow rose. Clusius indirectly started the tulipomania in Holland, when he priced his tulip bulbs too high and they were stolen. Clusius was the first to collect in the Balkans. Clusius gathered the first plant wealth from Spain and Portugal.

Ships, too, were returning from distant lands with floral curiosities and beauties. The Cape of Good Hope was beginning to contribute its Gladiolus, Amaryllids, Ornithogalums and curious succulents. Tropical Africa, too, contributed an occasional plant, brought back by the French expedition. The Far East, however, was still weakly represented, although the Hollyhock was present. Although the Jesuits were in Peking and the Dutch had established their long-term contact with Japan, generations were to pass before the really fine plants from the Far East would come to Europe.

The New World had contributed plants. Sweerts knew both sweet potatoes and Irish potatoes, tobacco, pineapples and peppers, but did not sell maize. In ornamentals he had already obtained seeds of two kinds of Sunflower, the Four-o'clock, African and French Marigolds (both really American), and had a few cactus plants.

Most of the plants that Sweerts carried are ornamentals—flowering bulbs, perennials, shrubs and a few annuals. A few food and economic plants, however, were available. Thus, in addition to the Tulips, Daffodils, Roses, Violets and Lilies which we would expect, there are also Eggplants, Tomatoes, Lemons and Oranges, Pomegranates, Belladonna and some legumes possibly intended for fodder. On the whole, however, the thrust of Sweerts's catalogue is toward novelty. These, for the most part, are the new plants of around 1600 or so, the unusual items that a wealthy nobleman or burgher would be proud to display uniquely in his area.

It is a little sad to add, though, that most of his plants have since slipped out of cultivation. Most of his standard garden plants have been superseded by superior varieties, and most of his carefully assembled bulbs from the Balkans and the Iberian Peninsula now exist only in the wild, or as rarities for the hyperspecialized rock gardener. His Scillas are not grown much now. His *Narcissus abscissus*, reported Grey in the 1930's, survives only on the daffodil mound in Kew. His *Tropaeolum minor* dropped completely out of cultivation, and when Tropaeolums were reintroduced, it was *Tropaeolum major*, our Nasturtium, that entered. Most of his perennials, too, are now plants for herbals, too old-fashioned for even old-fashioned gardens. Yet many of them still have charm, as seen in Sweerts's copperplates.

THIS EDITION

Besides his floral copperplates Sweerts also included considerable frontmatter. Largest in space is a series of eight detailed contents tables, in Latin, Dutch, German and French. These tables, which comprise 24 pages, give the name of the plant, color information and occasional secondary facts. I have incorporated this color data and more important secondary information into the legends at the back of the book. When the information is not exactly the same among the various languages, as is sometimes the case, I have followed the Dutch, since it was Sweerts's native language and most likely to convey his meaning.

I have also translated Sweerts's preface and advertisement, following the Dutch version when it differs from the French or German or Latin. For his gardening instructions, his German text has been followed, as opposed to the Latin, the only other version.

The following items have not been translated, since they seem of trivial interest to the reader: the official Octroy or copyright notice, signed by Count von Strahlendorff; a long, florid dedication to the new Emperor, Matthias (this would probably have been in vain even if Sweerts had lived, since Matthias was not interested in gardening); a French congratulatory sonnet by Augerius T. F. Clutius of Amsterdam; a Latin poem by Damasius Blyenburgius, Batavian; and a table of plants that Sweerts claimed to have introduced. None of these seemed likely to interest anyone but the specialist in botanical history, who would, in any case, consult an original edition.

All of Sweerts's plates have been reproduced from a fine copy of the first edition. After the plates a special section has been added detailing the modern botanical term and common name (where any exists) for each plant, as well as color indications based on the plates themselves and on Sweerts's contents pages, which do not always agree. Two points should be remembered about this color determination: first, these are not the total color possibilities for these plants, but Sweerts's holdings; second, they are more suggestive than precise. What Sweerts meant, exactly, by crimson or gray or brown is not always clear.

Only a rash man would dare to identify Sweerts's drawings down to the level of species. Genus is usually secure enough in the identifications that follow, but identifying species is sometimes a matter of guessing among a group of possibilities. It is not that Sweerts is any worse than the other plant illustrators of his day, just that his interest was the garden image of a plant. He was not concerned with the points that would involve a modern botanist, and data are often missing or misrepresented. To give two examples: a diagnostic feature for a Hyacinth, as opposed to a Scilla, is that the petals are fused; a means of distinguishing between various plants that look similar in flower—Crocuses, Colchicums, Sternbergias, Romuleas —is the nature of pistil and stamens. If all plants that look like Hyacinths are shown with unfused petals, if all plants that look like Crocuses are shown with closed flowers, the plant detective is hampered.

In many such cases an editor can rely on his general acquaintance with the gross appearance of the plants. Often this is adequate, so long as Sweerts or his sources did not conventionalize too much.

An editor can also attempt the historical path: to trace down the sources from which Sweerts took his illustrations, and work back down through the years. We have a fair knowledge of which plants Clusius introduced from the Balkans and Spain, and occasionally identification is possible via historical context. This, however, is a dangerous road.

These criticisms are not meant to imply that Sweerts is always inadequate. There are many fine touches supererogatory to a nursery catalogue. Care went into the drawings of the roots of the various Cyclamens, for example, and these are details that are significant botanically. Similarly, Sweerts bothered to record the foot on the Colchicum bulbs, the annulation on certain Crocus corms, and many similar small features.

The *Florilegium* has long been a neglected book in the history of botanical illustration. It is seldom mentioned in the literature, perhaps because it has no text, and it has been condemned for artistic deficiencies.

Both estimations, I believe, are unduly low. Sweerts's work is usually no worse than that of his more verbal contemporaries; it should also be remembered that he was compiling a catalogue platebook, not a botanical survey. From an aesthetic point of view, while he offers some bad plates, he also offers many plates that are fine. We do not know what happened to his business after his death, but his pictorial work still has elements of vitality even after three hundred and fifty years.

E. F. BLEILER

TRANSLATIONS

(Translation of original advertisement)

IF anyone wishes to purchase this book or the flowers, plants and bulbs that are contained in it, let him come at the time of the Fair to Frankfurt, to the author's shop opposite the Town Hall (the Römer). At other times, come to Amsterdam, to the shop of Paulus Aertssen van Ravensteyn, Book Printer.

(Translation of original preface)

TO THE GRACIOUS READER

 ENTLE READER: Since childhood, through a singular impulse of my spirit, I have taken pleasure not only in investigating but also in gathering and collecting all sorts of strange and wonderful natural creations of Almighty God, as well as the work of men's hands and the rarities which have been brought to our land on our ships, from the East and West Indies and the Northern and Southern regions and areas. Of all these things nothing has given me more pleasure than gazing at the manifold variety of the world of flowers. And so when I brought almost all sorts of plants to His Highest Born, Most Illustrious Majesty, the Late Emperor Rudolph the Second—His Imperial Majesty (who was the greatest, most enthusiastic admirer and lover of such things in the world, as well as of the arts), was pleased to order me to have them cut in copper and to arrange a book from them, and issue it, and graciously gave me his Privilege.

Thus His Majesty's pleasure first caused me to start this book. Also, while many highly learned men, both before us and in our own time, such as the most erudite and learned Dom. Rembertus Dodoneus, Dom. Matthias Lobell and the renowned Dom. Carolus Clusius (who in his last two books or parts of his herbary has described many strange foreign creatures—plants, animals, fishes and birds), have treated very learnedly of their essence and nature, and have depicted them very artistically, they have shown them in reduced size. For this reason amateurs have not been completely satisfied, and so I have taken pains not only to show the nature of the plants, but also the size of flower and bulb, with its color, as they ordinarily grow before our eyes.

My other cause and motivation for preparing this book has been to display with it, to all eyes, the infinite Power of God, in which one can look as in a mirror, and thereby be moved to understand how short and trivial life is; and on the other hand, how great is God's Mercy, since he shares with us worthless creatures His manifold beautiful, wonderful creations, the flowers, for our refreshment and comfort. These give us to know that man's life is nothing else than a flower of the fields, which withers soon, yet, according to the testimony of Christ, our Beloved Savior, is still more splendid than King Solomon in his greatest glory. Through them shall we be awakened and warned to laud and praise His Divine Goodness.

It has seemed well to divide this book into two parts. Thus, in the first part have been placed all flowers which have bulbs or tubers for roots, life-sized, with an indication of their diverse colors. I have also placed each sort on one page, as far as is possible, in accordance with their number, and named them. In the second part are to be seen plants with fibrous roots, each individual sort, as far as is possible, on a separate page, by which the lover of flowers can come best to the Key of Knowledge that Flora holds in her hand, and can prosper, for such a work as this has never before been brought to light or published.

Receive with gratitude, kind reader, this my book, prepared by my labor and at my expense, and I shall be moved to enlarge it according to my ability. May God be with you.

AMSTERDAM, 1 SEPTEMBER, 1612

(Translation of planting instructions)

SHORT INSTRUCTIONS FROM THE AUTHOR ON THE MANNER IN WHICH ONE SHOULD GO ABOUT PLANTING ALL SORTS OF BULBS

 ECAUSE I have been asked on many occasions in Germany, by certain eminent men and lovers of flowers and beautiful plants, to give them a good description of how one goes about lifting bulbs and resetting them, together with other matters, to be of service to these men, I am pleased to give the following information.

First, all flowers that have bulbs or tubers should be removed from the ground in August. However, take care that any plants that are setting seed stand until the seed is ripe.

Second, bulbs or tubers which have been lifted can be kept out of the ground for three weeks or a month without harm. They can also be restored to the ground within fourteen days or three weeks. The finer the earth is prepared, the better.

Third, the earth can be prepared and set to order in this manner and fashion. First, you must make a fairly large hole or pit; in it you must put one part of pure cow dung and one part of the best black soil and mix them together. Then you must let this stand for a good year's time, mingling them occasionally, so that weeds are destroyed and the cow dung becomes rotted. Then you will have good soil.

Fourth, you can also prepare good soil for yourself in this fashion. Take old tanner's bark, such as the shoemakers use, the older the better, and to it add good black earth. Put it in a pit and mix it together, as described. Let it lie through the year until the bark is rotted, and then take this soil and rub it through a sieve. If you set flowers and plants in it, they will grow beautifully.

FLORILEGIVM
EMANVELIS SWEERTI SEPTIMON,
TI BATAVI AMSTELEDAMI COMORANTIS, TRA
CTANS DE VARIIS FLORIB, ET ALIIS INDICIS PLÃ
TIS AD VIVVM DELINEATVM IN DVABVS
PARTIB, ET QVATVOR LINGVIS
CONCINNATVM.

PROSTAT VENALI TVNA
CVM, FLORIB, ET PLANTIS,
IPSIS, APVD IPSVM AVTOREM, EMAN,
SWEERTIVM CVIVS OFFICINA ANTE
CVRIAM, FRANCOFVR M DC XII.

CAROLVS CLVSIS.

REMBERTVS DODONÆVS.

Impressum Francofurti ad Mœnum Apud Anthonium Kempner sumptib, Autoris. 1 6 92.

1   Crown Imperials.

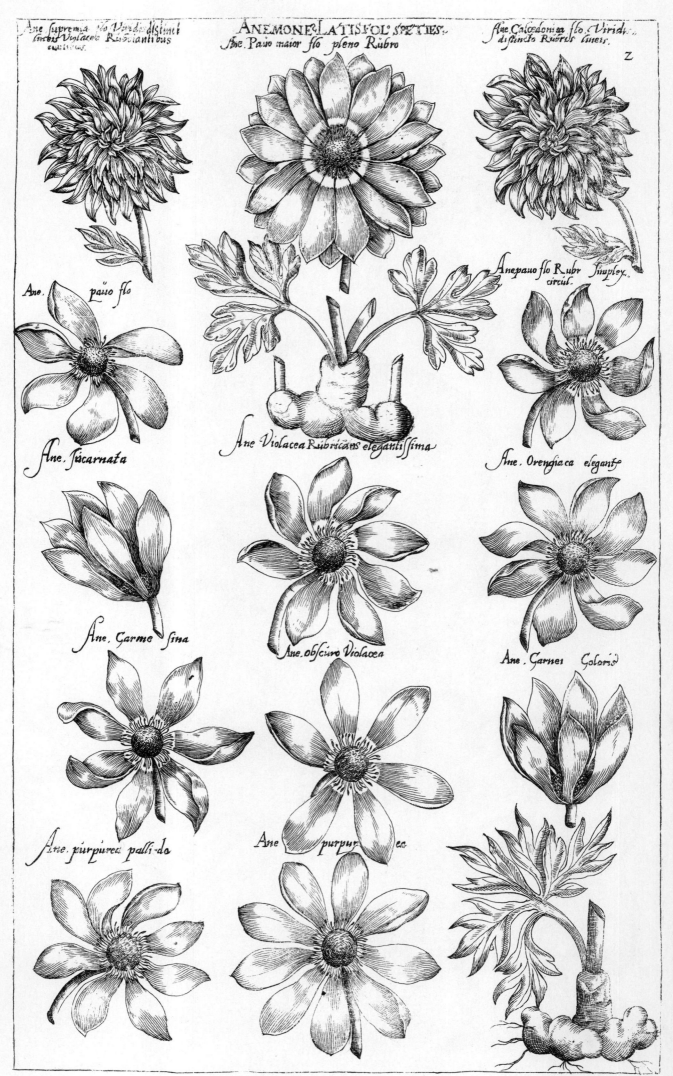

Ane supremia flo Viridi distinct
lineis Violaceis Rubicantibus

ANEMONE LATISFOL SPETIES
Ane. Pauo maior flo pleno Rubro

Ane Calcedonia flo Viridi
distincto Rubris lineis

Ane. pauo flo

Anepauo flo Rubr simplex
circul.

Ane. Incarnata

Ane Violacea Rubricans elegantissima

Ane. Orengiaca elegante

Ane. Garme sina

Ane. obscuro Violacea

Ane. Garnei Coloris

Ane. purpurea palli do

Ane purpurea

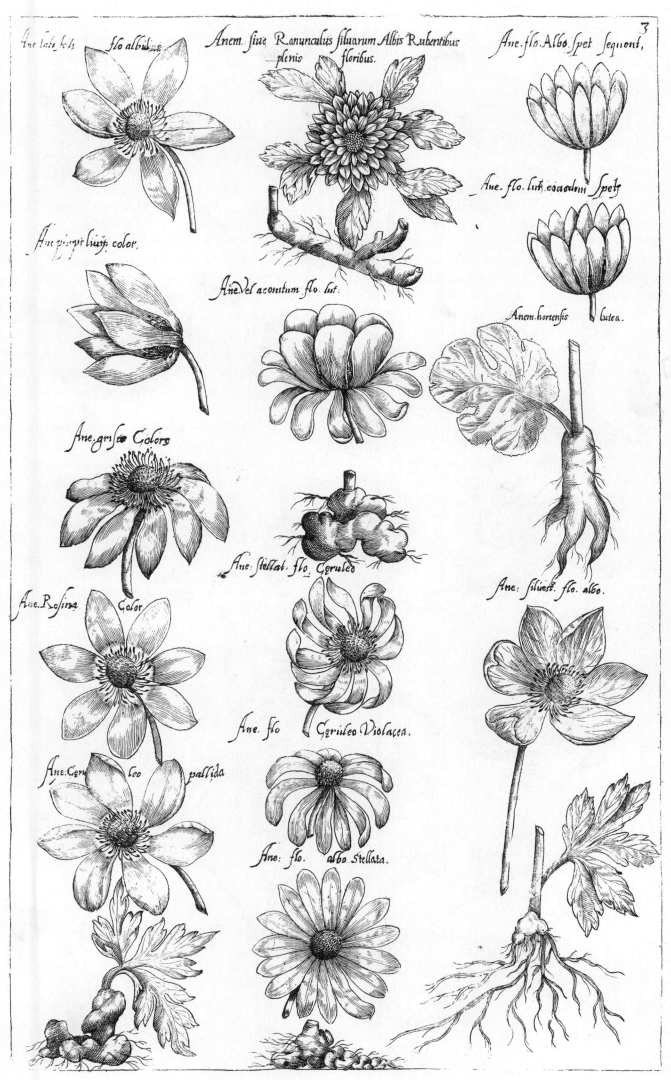

Ane late foli flo albidine

Anem. sive Ranunculus siluarum Albis Rubentibus plenis floribus.

Ane. flo. Albo. spet sequent,

Ane pimps liuip color.

Ane. Vel aconitum flo. lut:

Ane. flo. lut. eoasdun Spet:

Anem. hortensis lutea.

Ane. griso Colore

Ane: Stellat. flo. Ceruleo

Ane: siluest. flo. albo.

Ane. Rosina Color

Ane. flo Ceruleo Violacea.

Ane. Cerru leo pallida

Ane: flo. albo Stellata.

3 Anemones and Other Plants.

4 Anemones.

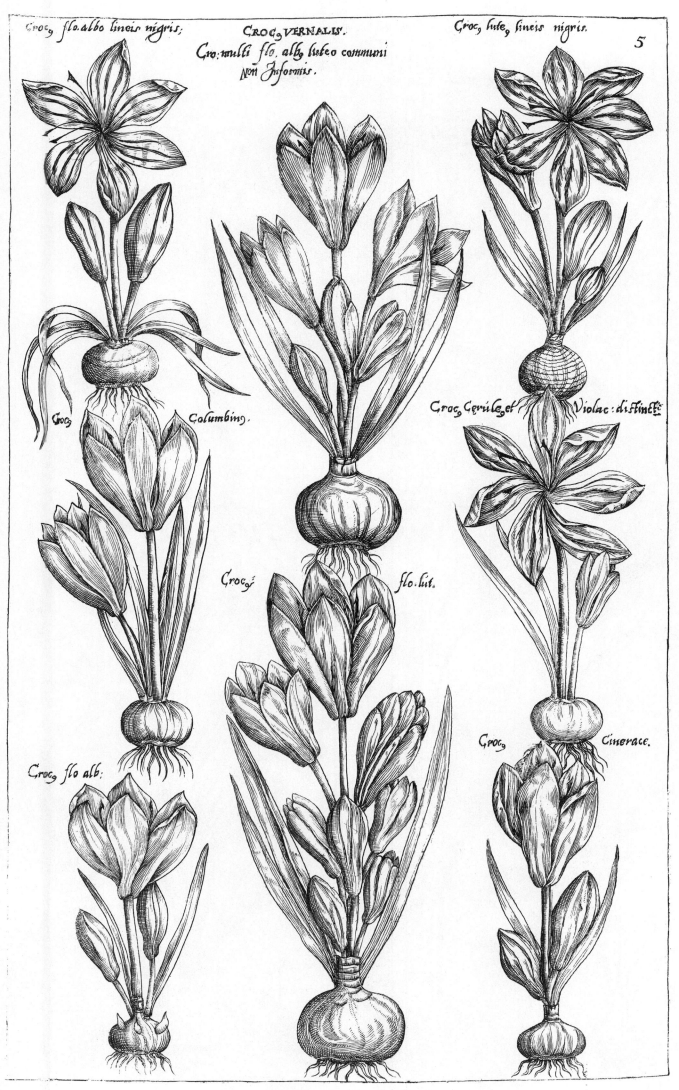

Croc. flo. albo lineis nigris.

CROC. VERNALIS.
Cro: multi flo. alb. luteo communi
Non Informis.

Croc. lute. lineis nigris.

Croc.   Columbin.

Croc. Cerule. et   Violac: distinct.

Croc.   flo. lut.

Croc. flo. alb:

Croc.   Cinerace.

Crocus Cæruleus Distinctus lineis Violaceis.

Crocus Columbinus.

Dens Caninus flo.

Dens Caninis Alba flo.

6

Crocus Cineraceus.

Crocus verus purpi. Color.

Crocus purpureo Rubens:

Crocus Cærul, Violaceus

Colchicum pannonicum Alba flore.

6 Autumn-Flowering Crocuses and Similar Plants.

frittilla: Aquitanica flo luto obscuro

frittillariae Minimae

frittillaria Hispanica Vmbellifera

Frittillaria Vulgaris purpureo Colore

frittillariae Alb flore

Frittillariae

flore Luto

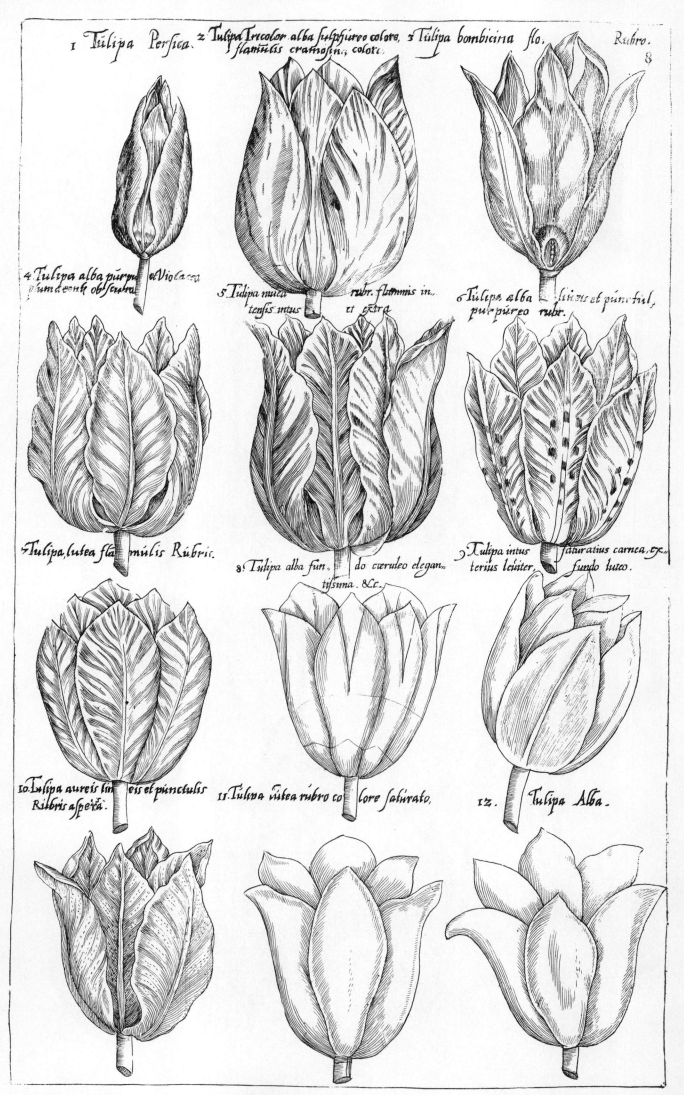

1 Tulipa Persica. 2 Tulipa Tricolor alba sulphureo colore, 3 Tulipa bombicina flo. Rubro.
flammulis cramosina colore

8

4. Tulipa alba purpur. et Violacea
plum deante obscura

5 Tulipa nivea   rubr. flammis in..
tensis intus   et extra

6 Tulipa alba   liteis et punctul,
purpureo rubr.

7 Tulipa, lutea fla mulis Rubris.

8 Tulipa alba fun.   do cœruleo elegan..
tissima. &c.

9 Tulipa intus   saturatius carnea, ex..
terius leuiter.   fundo luteo.

10. Tulipa aureis lin eis et punctulis
Rubris aspersa.

11 Tulipa lutea rubro co   lore saturato,

12.   Tulipa Alba.

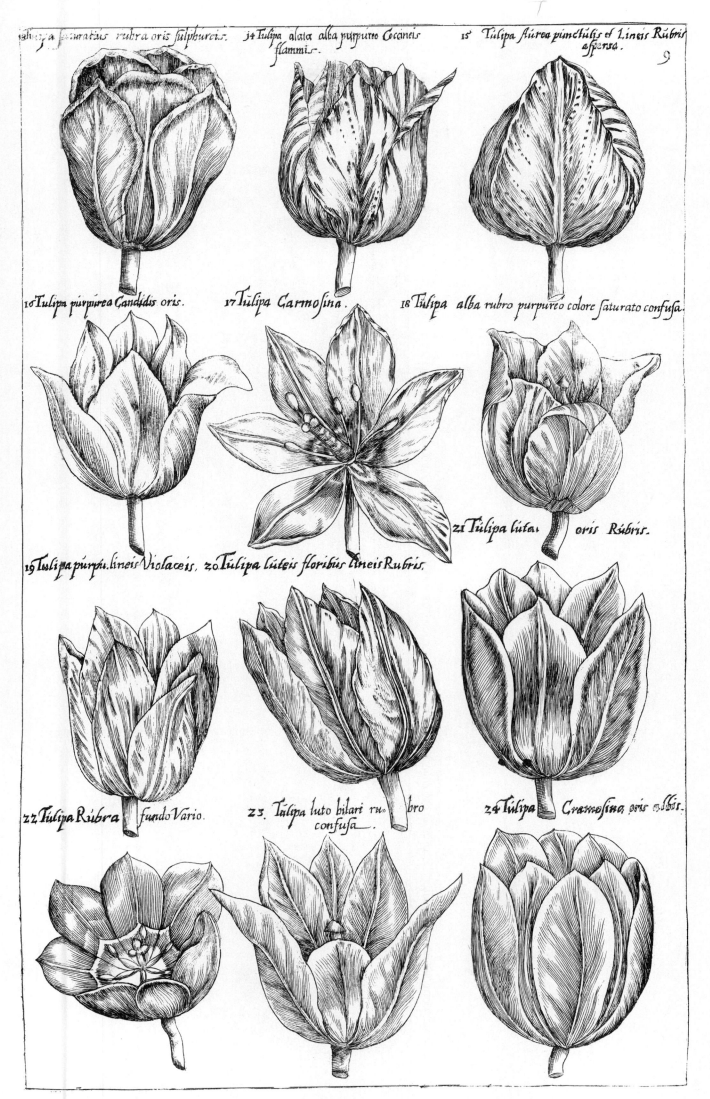

13 Tulipa saturatius rubra oris sulphureis. 14 Tulipa alata alba purpureo Coccineis flammi. 15 Tulipa Aurea punctulis et Lineis Rubris aspersa.

16 Tulipa purpurea Candidis oris. 17 Tulipa Carmosina. 18 Tulipa alba rubro purpureo colore saturato confusa.

19 Tulipa purpu. lineis Violaceis. 20 Tulipa luteis floribus lineis Rubris. 21 Tulipa lutea oris Rubris.

22 Tulipa Rubra fundo Vario. 23 Tulipa luto bilari rubro confusa. 24 Tulipa Cramosina oris albis.

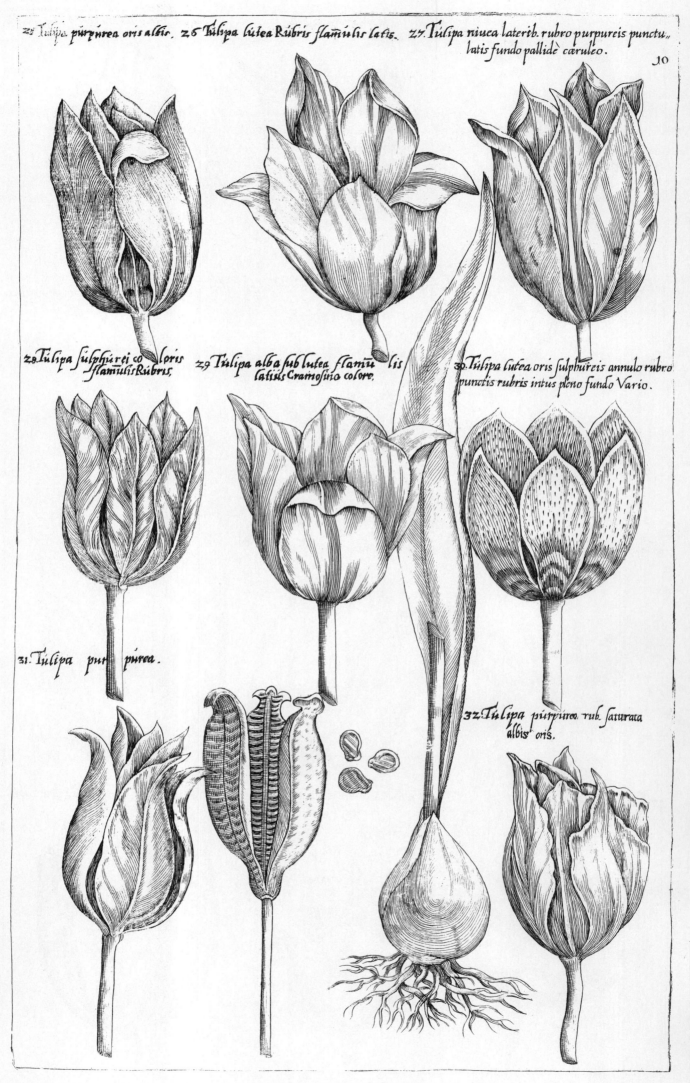

24. Tulipa purpurea oris albis.   26. Tulipa lutea Rubris flamulis latis.   27. Tulipa niuca laterib. rubro purpureis punctu=
latis fundo pallidè cæruleo.

28. Tulipa sulphurei coloris flamulis Rubris.   29. Tulipa alba sub lutea flamulis latis Cramosino colore.   30. Tulipa lutea oris sulphureis annulo rubro punctis rubris intus pleno fundo Vario.

31. Tulipa purpurea.

32. Tulipa purpurea rub. saturata albis oris.

*Hya: orient: precox multi.
flo: cerulē.*

Hya:orient flo: albo.

Hya:orient serotin, flo:purpū:

Hya.orient flo.albicante

*Hya faue orientalis
flo:albo*

*Hya facie orien
tal: flo:cer ideo*

Hya.orient flo.albicante

11   Hyacinths and Similar Plants.

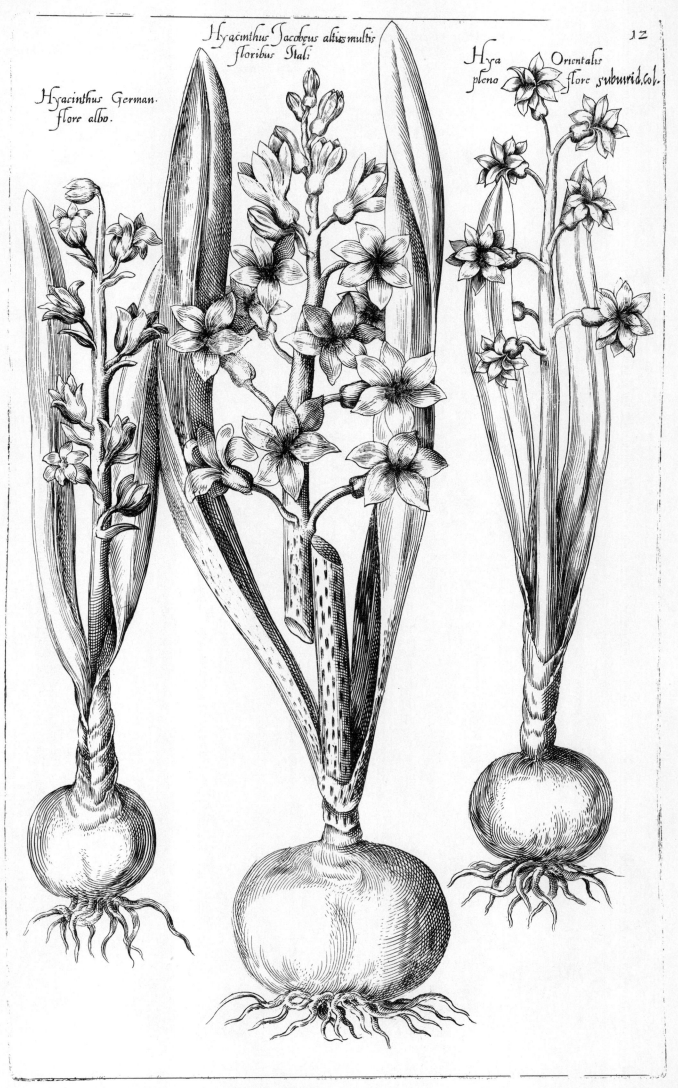

Hyacinthus German.
flore albo.

Hyacinthus Jacobeus altius multis
floribus Itali

Hya   Orientalis
pleno   flore suburrid. Col.

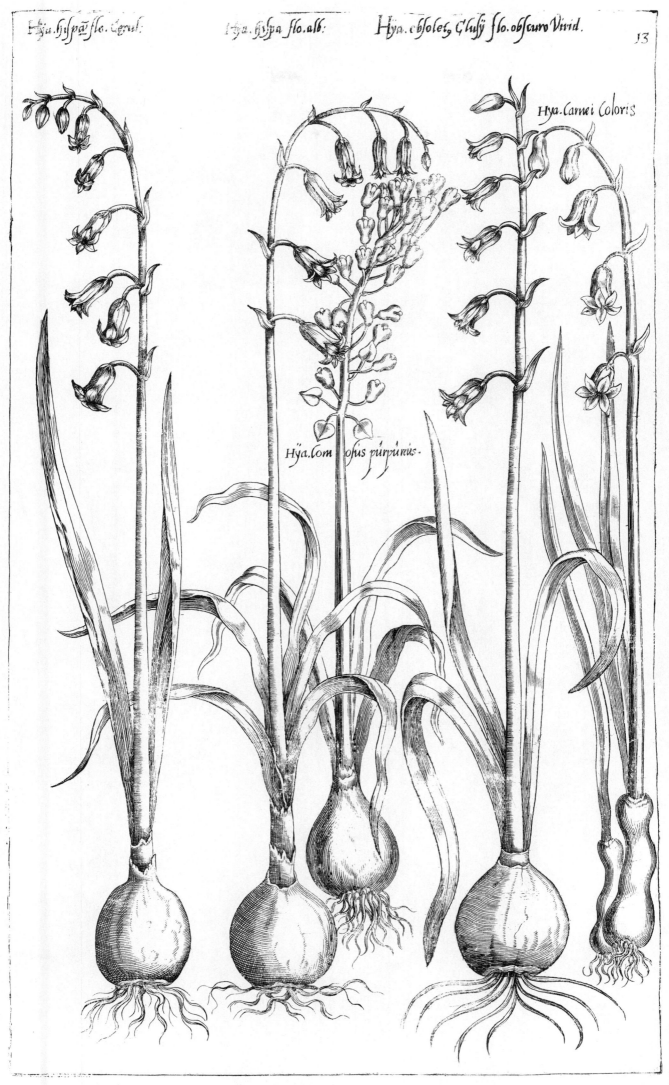

Hya.Carnei Coloris

Hya.Com posis purpurus.

Hya. maior Indici tuberosa Radice, non descriptus.

Hya. minor Indici tuberosa Radice, albus.

34

Hya. Indici minima, orienta dicti, Swertius.

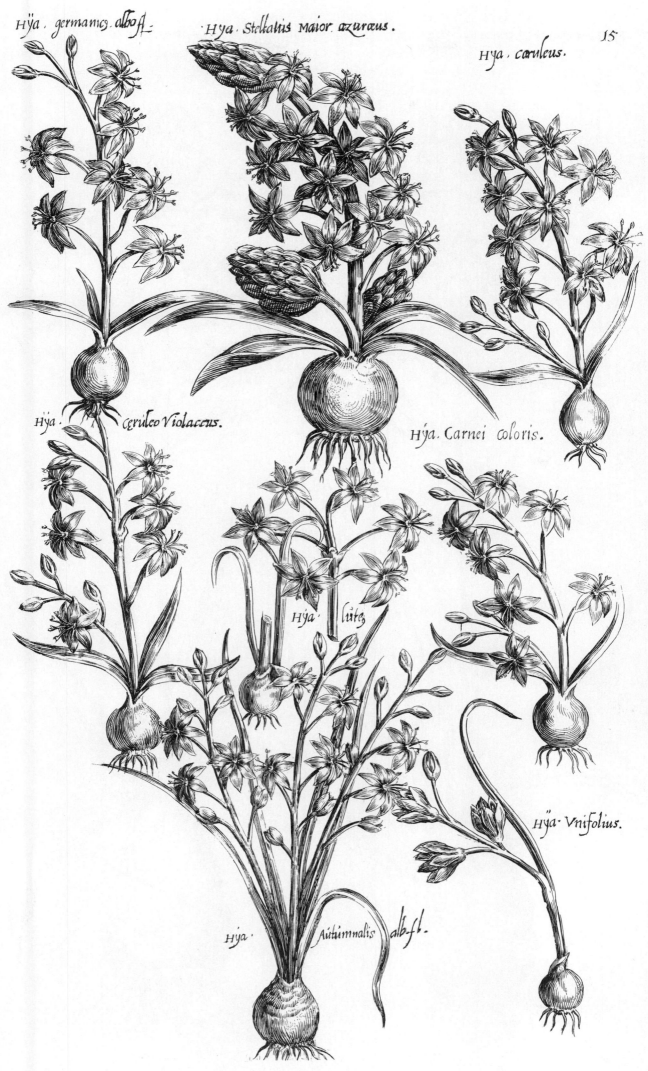

Hÿa. germanic9. albo.fl.　　Hya. Stellatis Maior. azureus.

Hya. ceruleus.

Hÿa. Ceruleo Violaceus.　　Hÿa. Carnei coloris.

Hÿa. lute.

Hÿa. Vnifolius.

Hÿa. Autumnalis albo.fl.

15　Bulbous Plants.

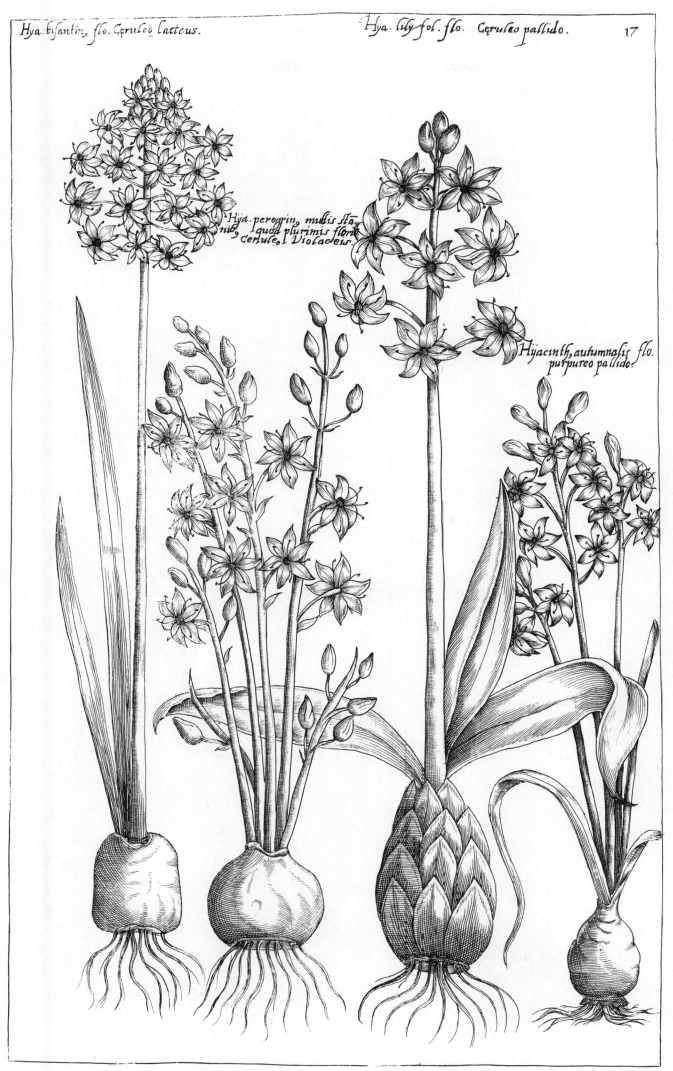

Hya. peregrin. multis sta-
mib, quod plurimis florib
Cœruleo Violaceis.

Hyacinth, autumnalis flo.
purpureo pallido.

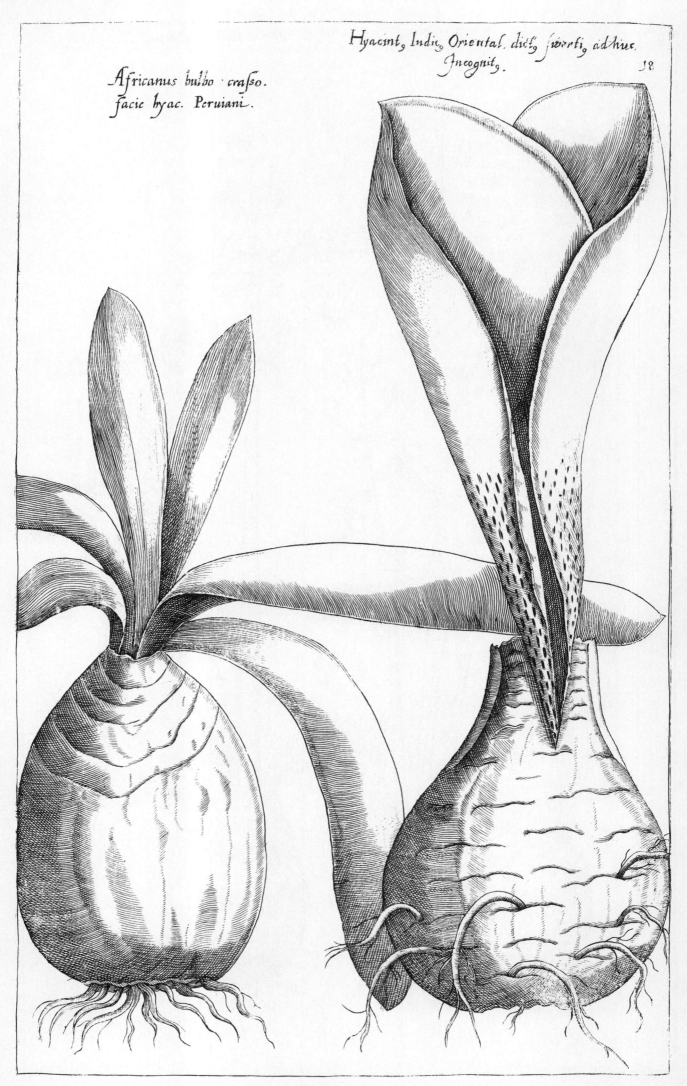

Africanus bulbo · crasso.
facie hyac. Peruiani.

Hyacint, Indic, Oriental. diff, sortis ad huc.
Incognit,

18

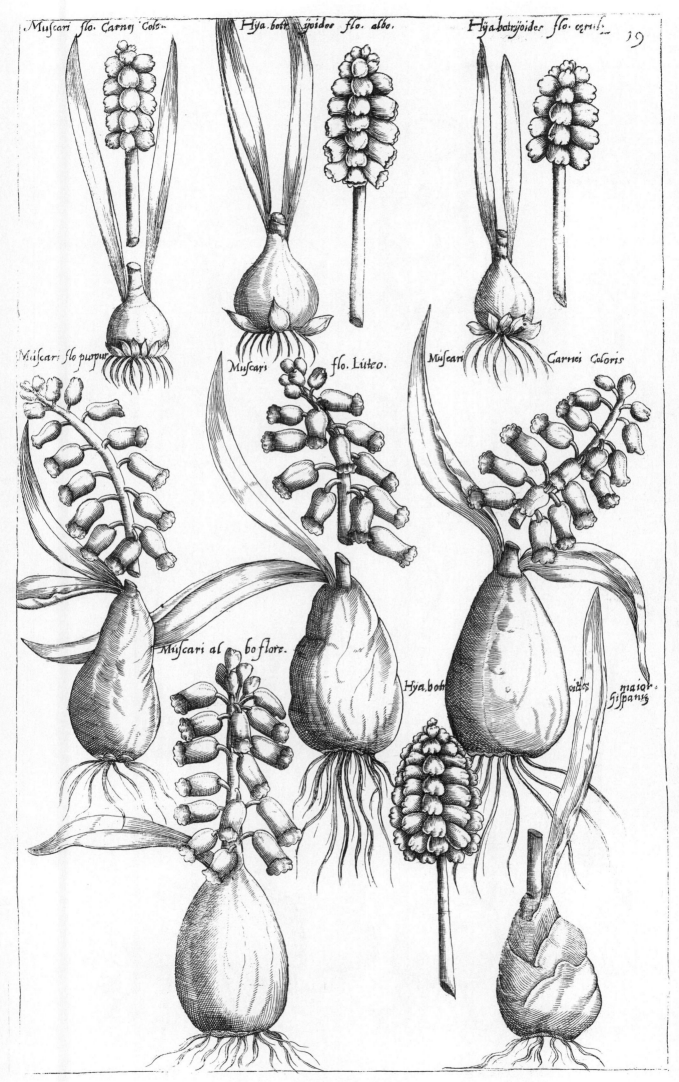

Muscari flo. Carnes Cols.

Hya. botr. ijoides flo. albo.

Hÿa. botrijoides flo. cæril.

Muscari flo purpur.

Muscari flo. Luteo.

Muscari Carnei Coloris

Muscari al bo flore.

Hya. botr. oides maior Hispanic

Narcif. leucoiū maior hiſpaie

Nar. leucoiū bohemī

Nar hiſpa. leucoium minor

Nar germanie vulgaris

Nar. leucoium autumnalis

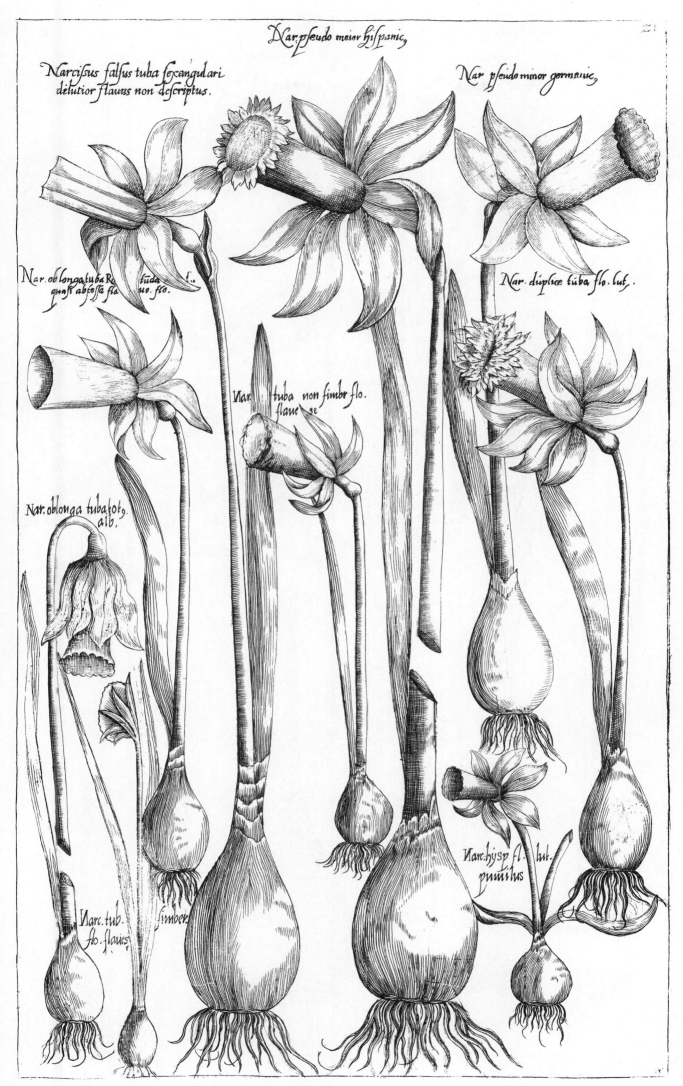

Nar.pseudo maior hispanic.

Narcissus falsus tuba sexangulari delutior flauus non descriptus.

Nar. pseudo minor germanic.

Nar. oblonga tuba Ro tuda quasi abscissa fla uo. flo.

Nar. duplice tuba flo. lut.

Nar tuba non fimbr flo. flaue se

Nar. oblonga tuba fot. alb.

Narc. tub. flo. flaues

fimber

Narc. hysp fl. lut. pumilus

21 Narcissus.

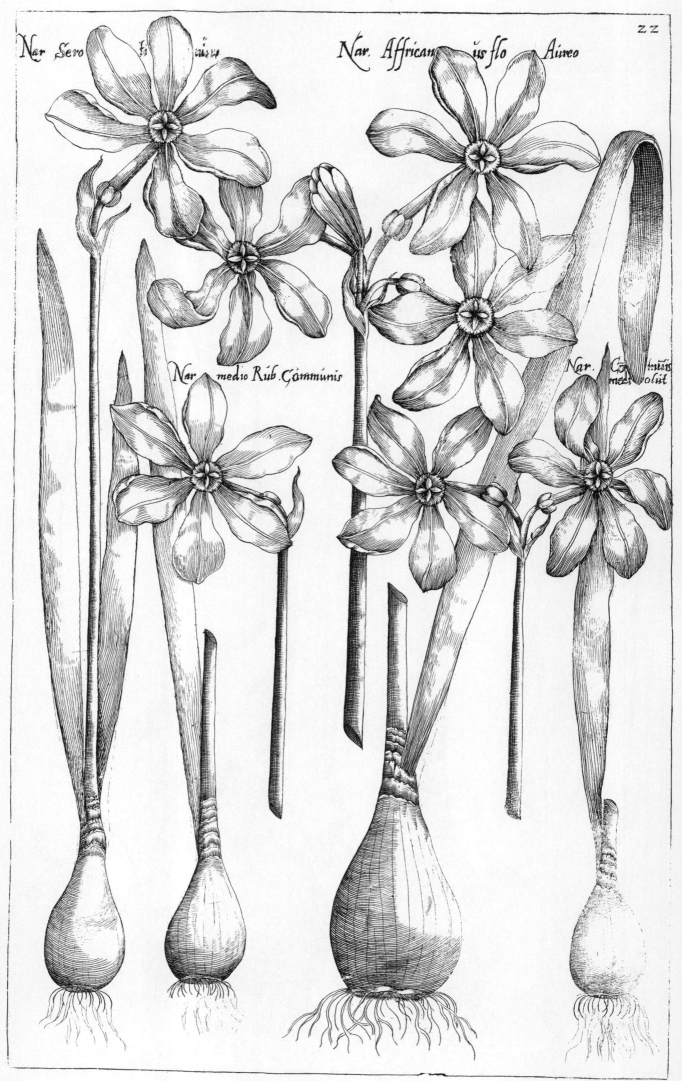

Nar. Sero Hispanicus

Nar. Africanius flo Aureo

Nar. medio Rub. Communis

Nar. Communis medi oluit

, *Narciss. Aureus Aphrican. Maior multi flor. Coronat.*

Narciss. maior medio luteus ex Italia.

3 . *Narciss. medio lute. Donax Narbonensis.*

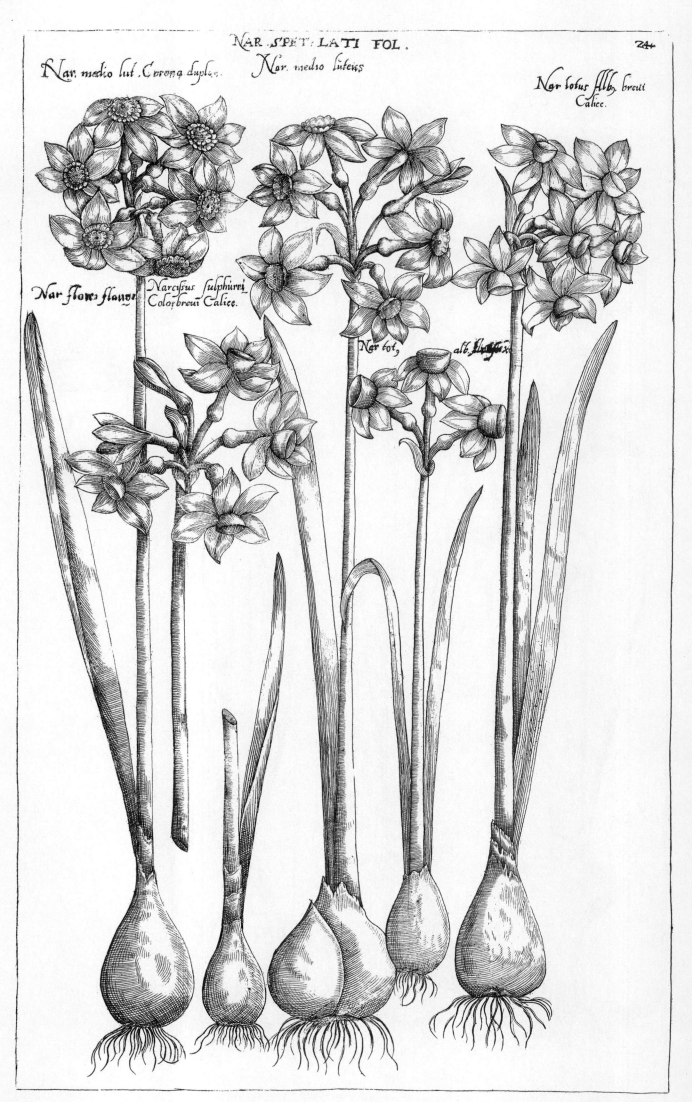

NAR. SPET. LATI FOL.

Nar. medio lut. Corona dupl. Nar. medio luteus

Nar. totus alb, breui Calice.

Nar flores flauo. Narcissus sulphurei Colo: breui Calice.

Nar tot, alb. flu

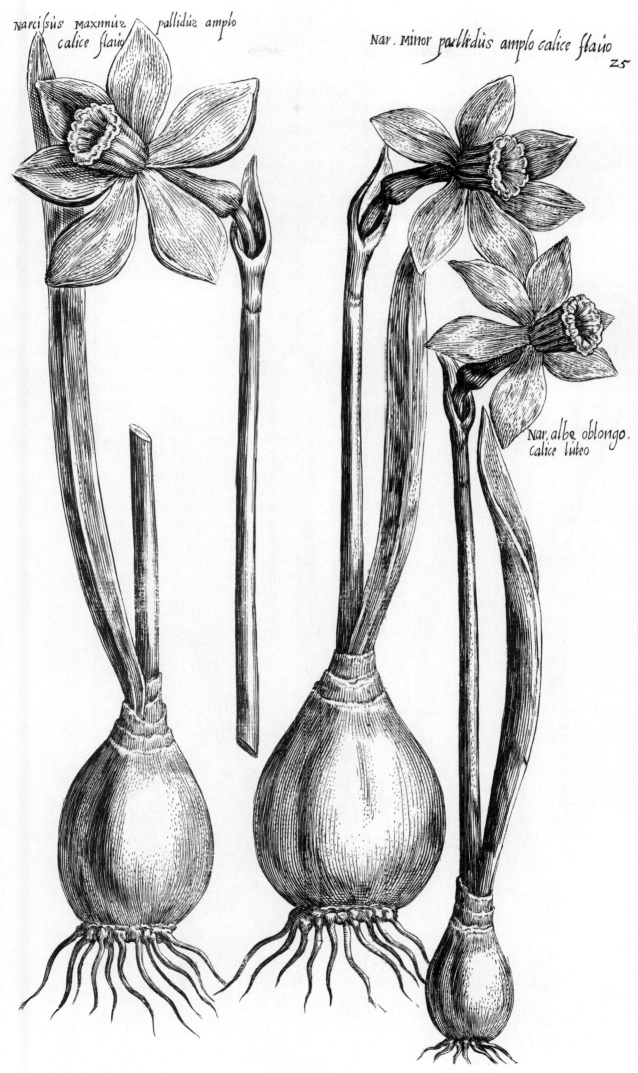

Narcissus Maxnnus pallidus amplo calice flauo

Nar. Minor pallidus amplo calice flauo

25

Nar. albe oblongo. calice luteo

Nar. Calcedonica pleno flore albo.

Pseudonarcissus duplex diuiso
calice odoratus.

Pseudonarc. luteus flauo pleno flore.

Nar. flauo pleno flore.

Narcis. Albo pleno fl.

Nar. tertius Mathioli multi flo. alb.   *Nar. Pancratius marinus flo. alb.*

2ᵃ SPETIES LATI FOLIA APRECEDENT℮„
differens
Nar. Indicus dict, flo. Janguine,

Nar a D. Caret, flo alb. exteriori
parte Rubicundo

Narbornus flo. luty

NARCIS IVNCIS FOLIS.

Nar. Luteus distinctu
lineis albis

Nar. Au.   reus
pleno.   flore.

Nar. flo. Luteo breue
Calicem.

Nar. totg alb, Re..
flexo

Nar. maxi   mo   Calicem
flo   lut.

Nar. ob lon   go calice
flo.   lu...   9

29   Mostly Jonquils.

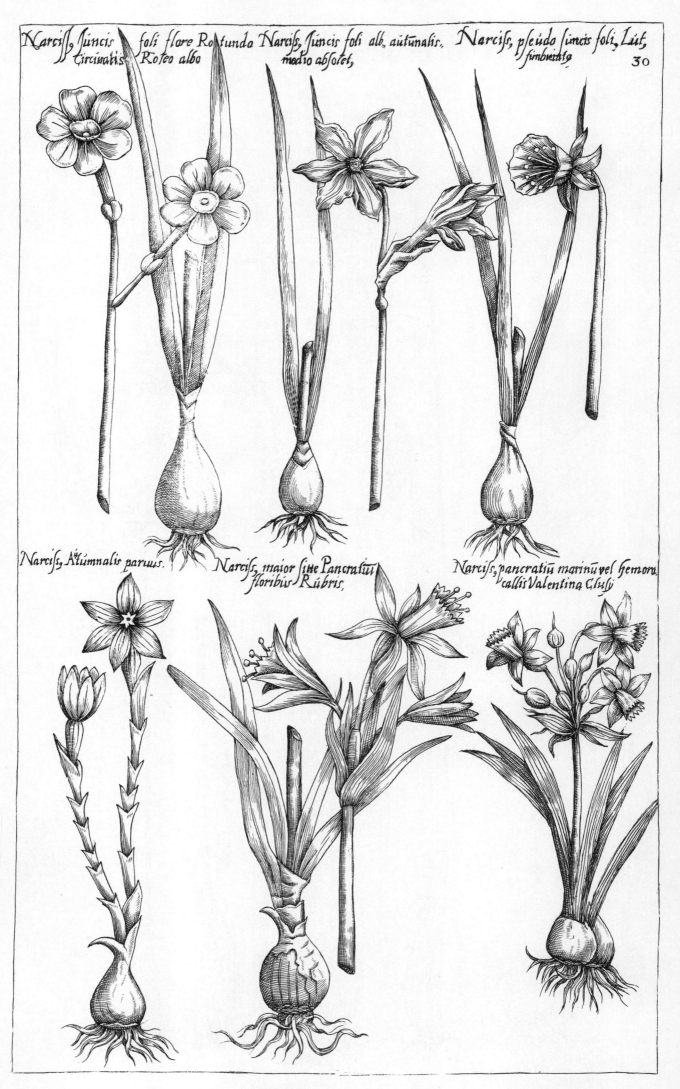

Narciss Juncis foli flore Rotundo Narciss, Juncis foli alb, autunalis. Narciss, pseudo Juncis foli, List, Circinalis, Roteo albo medio absolet, fimbriatis

30

Narciss, Autumnalis paruus. Narciss, maior siue Pancratiu floribus Rubris, Narciss, pancratiu marinu vel Hemora callis Valentina Clusi

30 Narcissus and Other Plants.

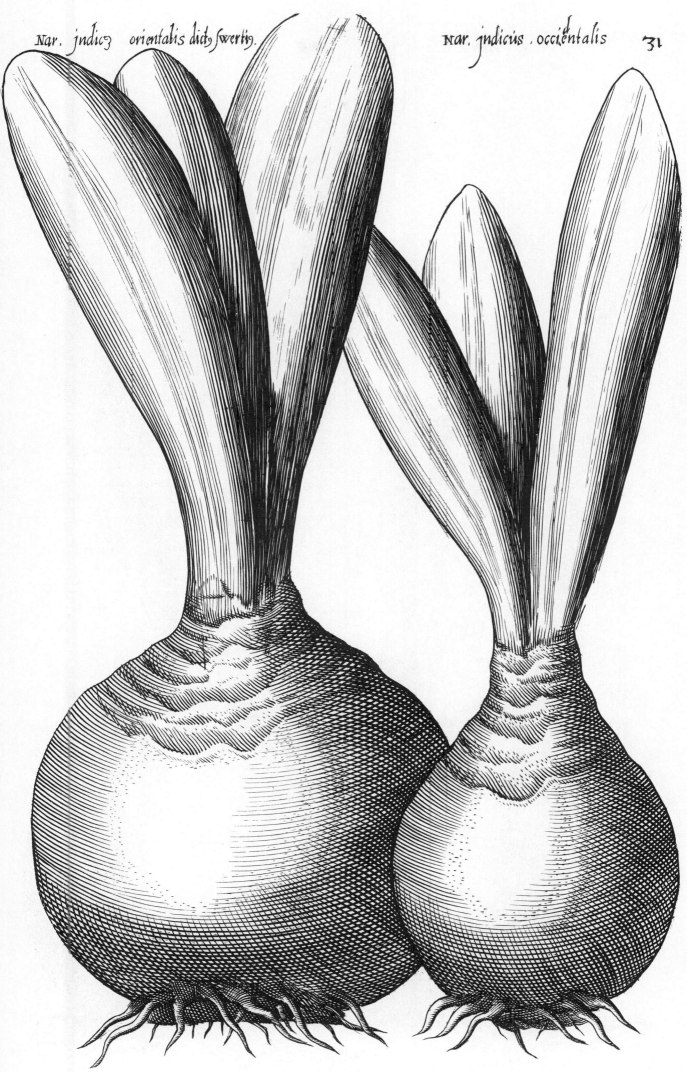

Nar. ſiue pancralium oriental.   Nar. ſiue   pancralium occidental.

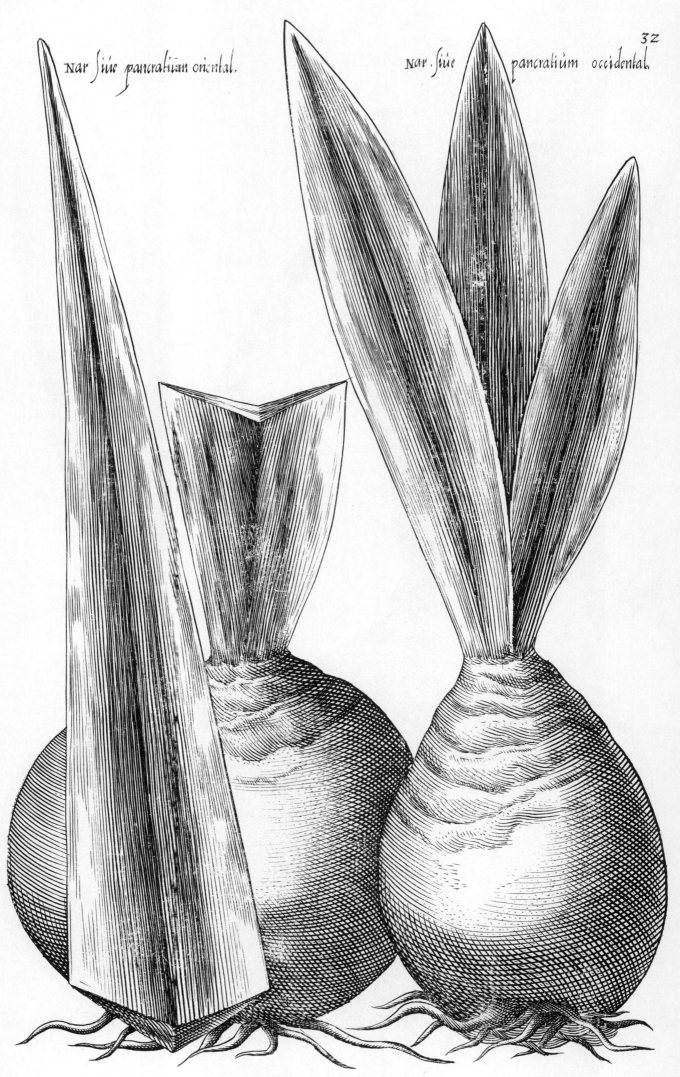

scilla marina.

Nar. siue pancratiū maius Hispa. 33ᵃ

Nar. scilla Minor.

nar. siue pancratium clusij.

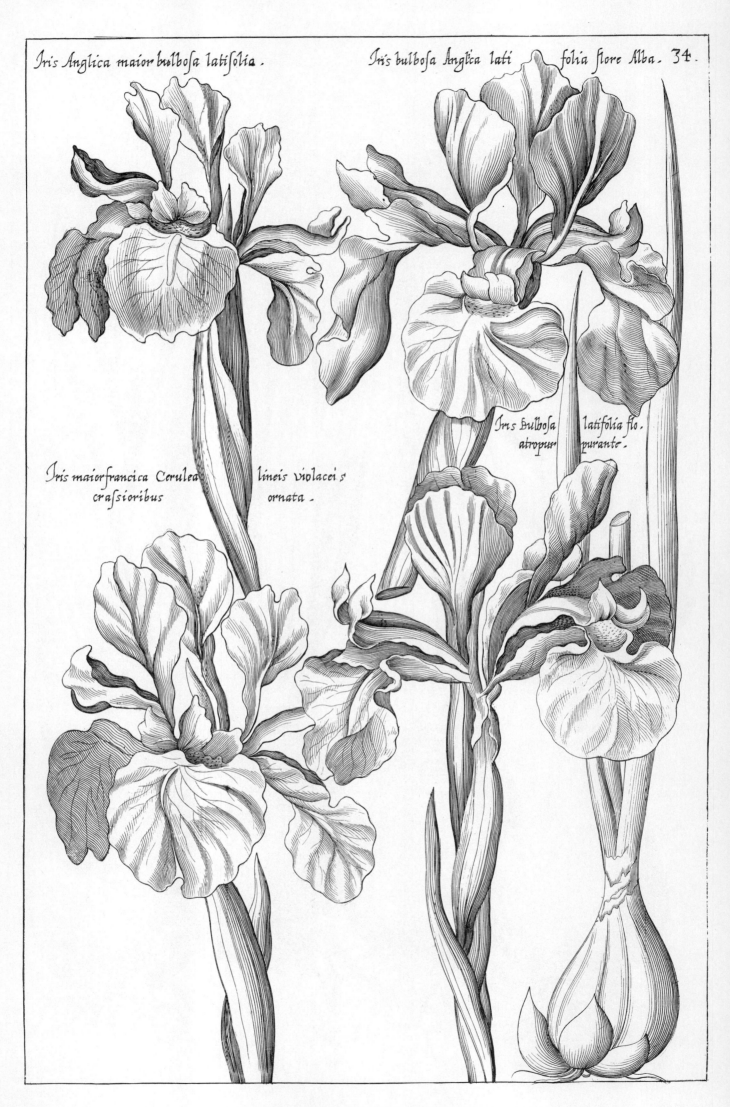

Iris Anglica maior bulbosa latifolia.

Iris bulbosa Anglica lati folia flore Alba. 34.

Iris bulbosa latifolia flo. atropur purante.

Iris maior francica Cerulea crassioribus lineis violaceis ornata.

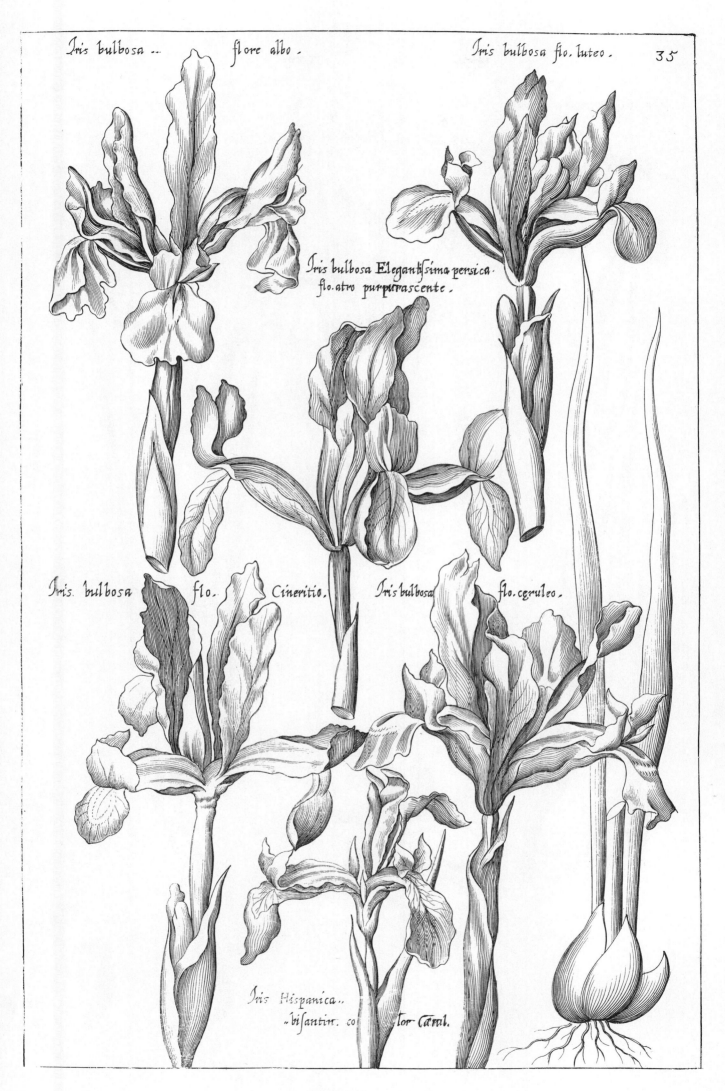

Iris bulbosa . . . flore albo .

Iris bulbosa flo. luteo .

Iris bulbosa Elegantissima persica . flo. atro purpurascente .

Iris. bulbosa flo. Cineritio .

Iris bulbosa flo. cæruleo .

Iris Hispanica . . . bisantin. co . . . tor Cærul.

gris Hispanica cærul. purpur.

gris bulbosa Latifolia purpu.

gris tuberosa obscuro viridi Colo.

Iris bisantina Aug fol Cærul   gris Hispanica maior august fol   gris Hispanica fl. Cæruleo. 37
fl pleno   fl alb

Iris bisantina Aug fol Cærul   gris Hispanica maior august   gris minima purp Hispanica Color. Cæruleo. 37

37   Irises.

Iris. Exotica Camerary.   Iris Susiana maior variegata.

Iris Susiana latifol. min.
sat. cum maiore. Eadem.

Iris latifol. atro, purpurea.

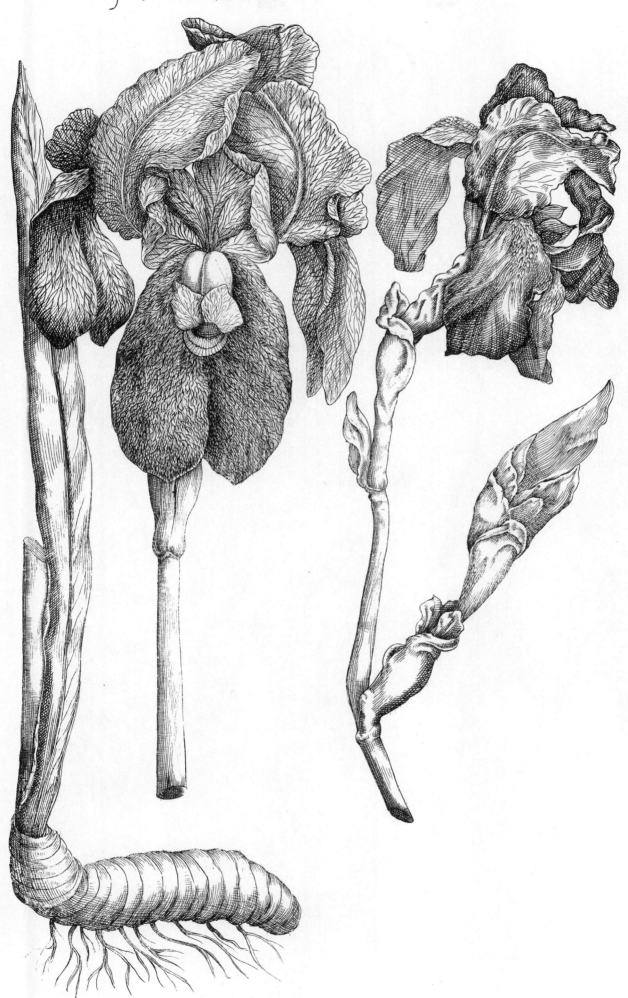

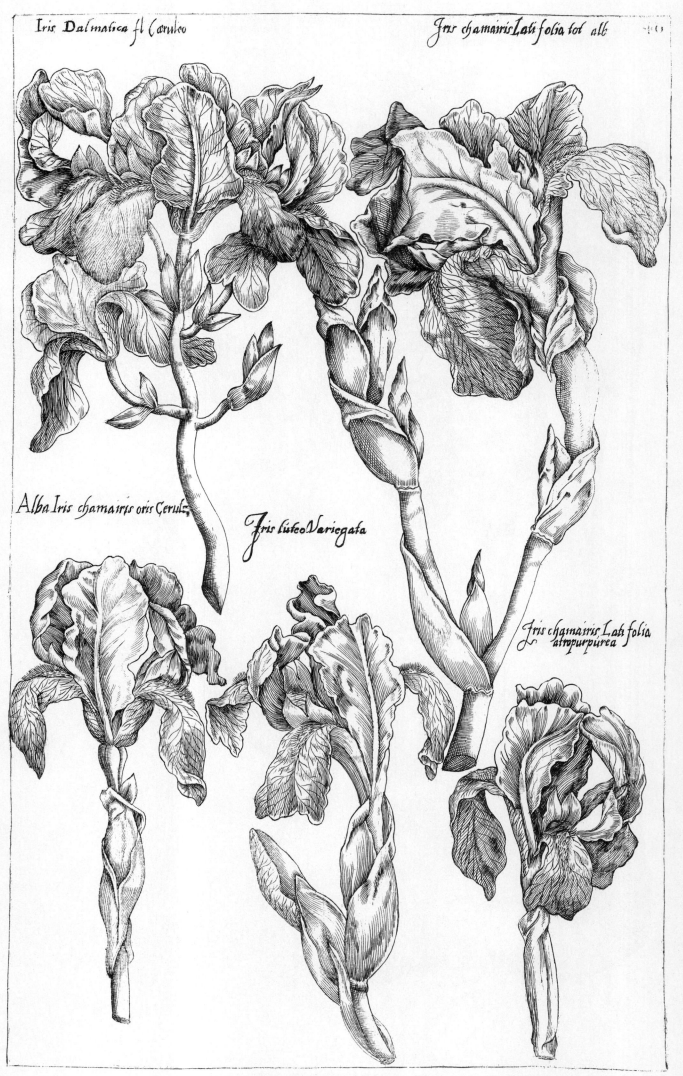

Iris Dalmatica fl Caruleo

Iris chamairis Latifolia tot alb

Alba Iris chamairis oris Ceruls

Iris luteo Variegata

Iris chamairis Latifolia atropurpurea

40 Bearded Irises.

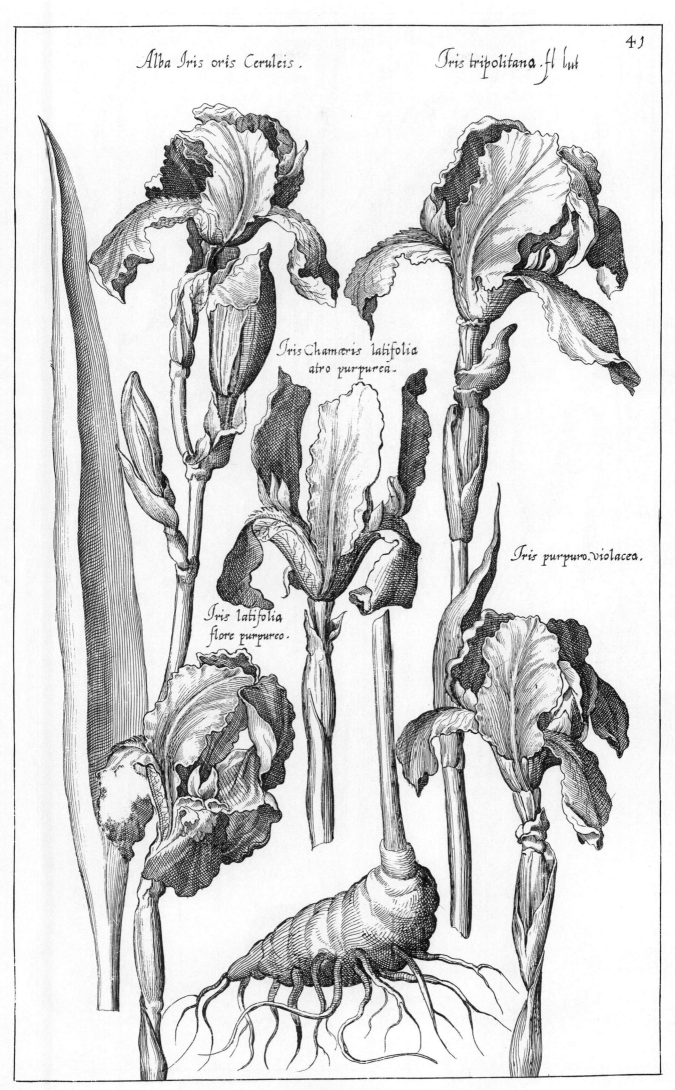

Alba Iris oris Ceruleis.

Iris tripolitana. fl lut

Iris Chamæris latifolia
atro purpurea.

Iris purpuro. violacea.

Iris latifolia
flore purpureo.

41 Bearded Irises.

Gladiolꝰ bisantinus atro purpurꝰ   Gladiolꝰ flo. albo.

Gladiolꝰ Carnei
Color

Gladiolꝰ Italicꝰ
purpuro.Violacꝰ

Dracuncul, vel   serpentaria maior.

Arum maius

Arum minus an-
gusti fol.

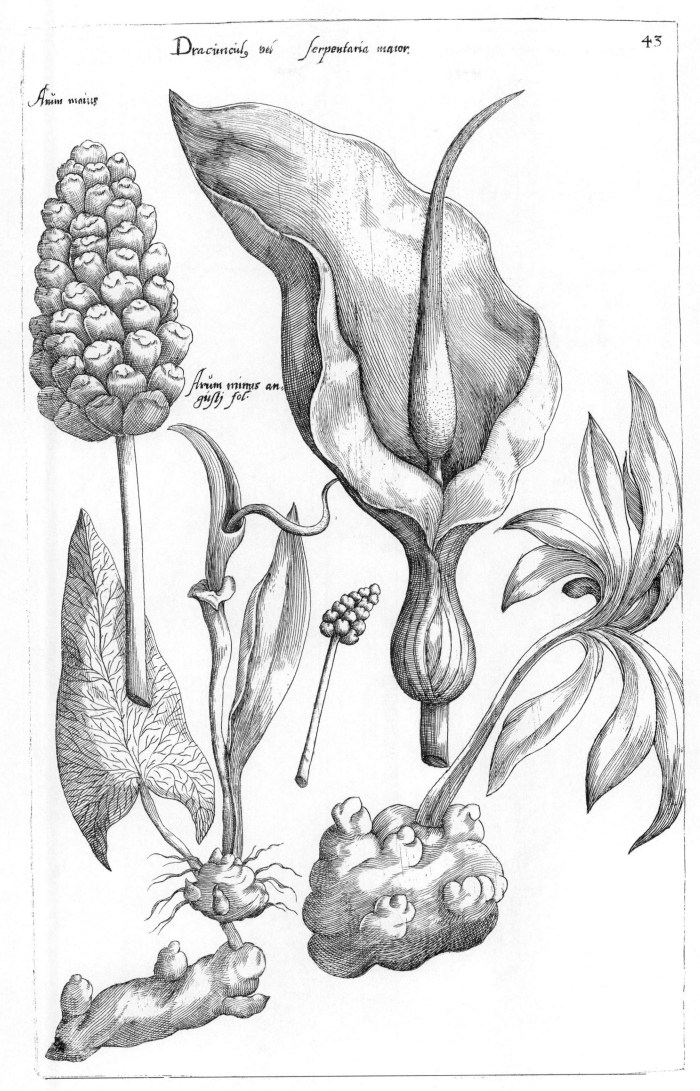

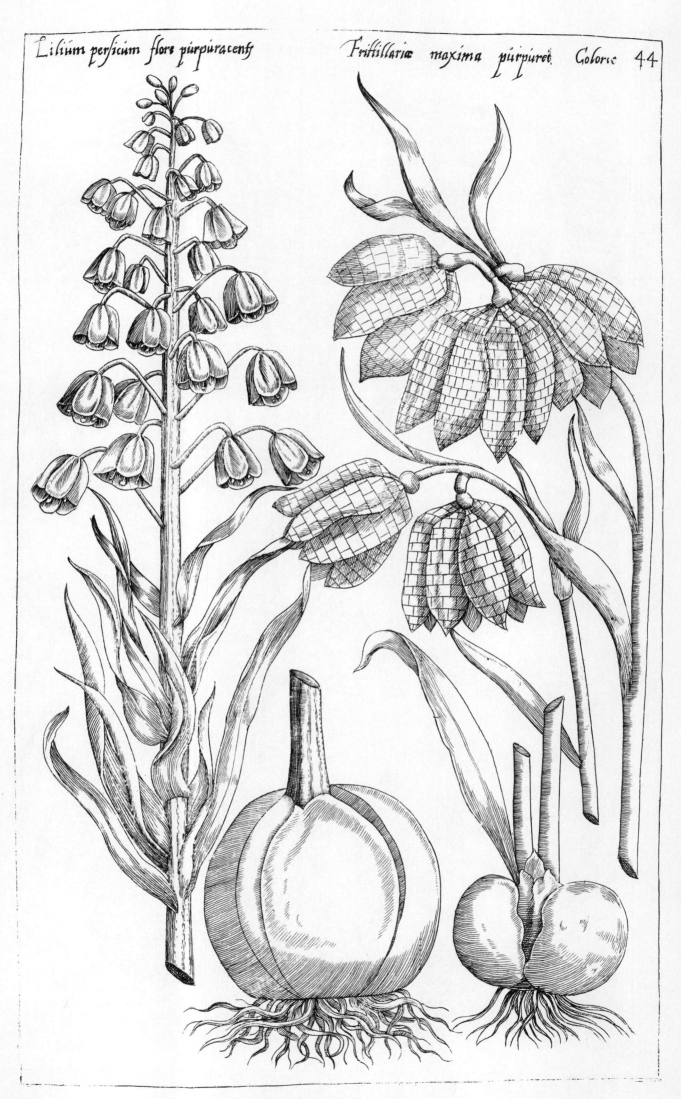

Lilium flo. Alb.   Lilium bifantinum.

Lilium flore. flauo.

lilium. rubrum bulbiferum.

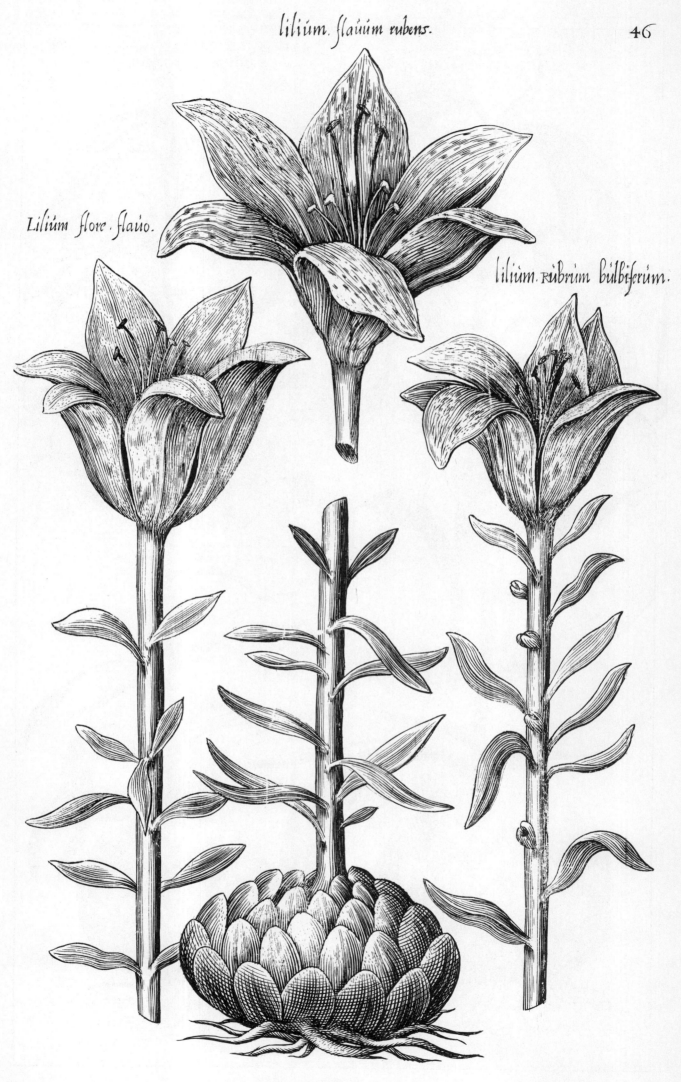

Liliosphodel, Lute,

Phalengium Asbrosicium parui lily forma.

Liliosphodel, flore Rubro.

Asphodelus Ramosus fl. albo.   Asphodelus luteus.   Asphodelus minor flore albo.

Martagon pomponij praecox multiflorum.   Martagon Calce — donicumpaucioribus
flo. ri. bus.

Martagon multis et magnis
foribus luteis alios superans

Martagon flauo sub viridi color.

Martagon ſiue Hemorocallis flo.
Albicante.

Martagon. ſiue Hemorocallis ſuaui.
flo. Rubente.

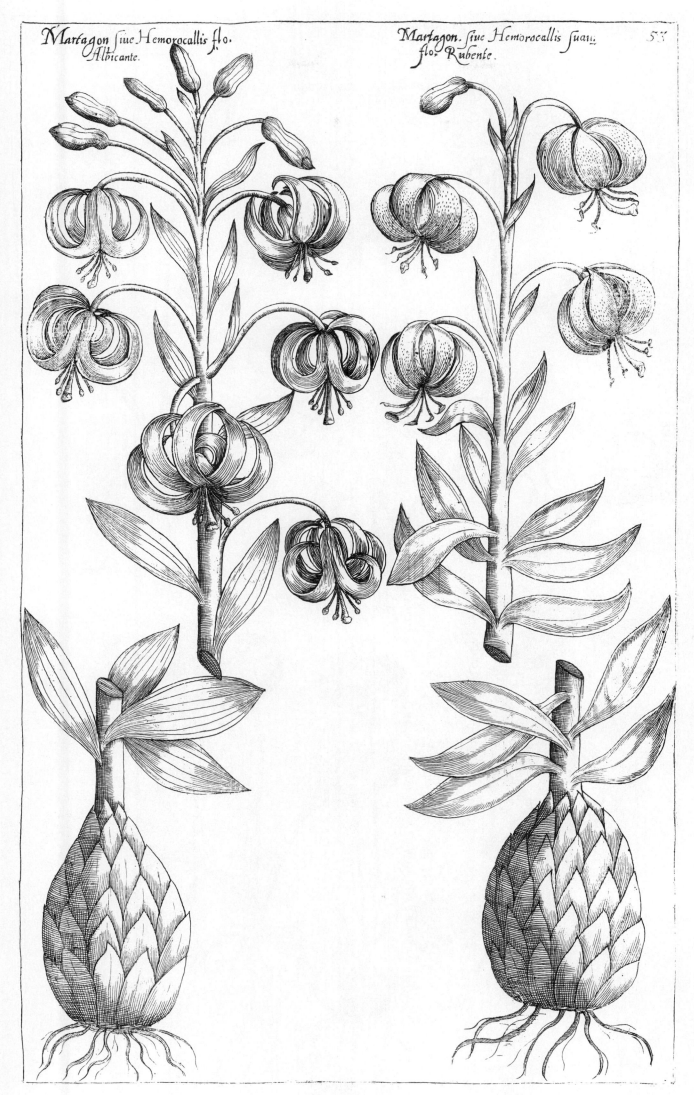

Raminail, Lusitanicus
clusy.

Ranunc. grum. Radice flo. Rub.   Ranunc. Asiat grum. Radi. flo. alb. Rubi.

Ranunail,   magnus Anglic,
pleno flor.   luteo.

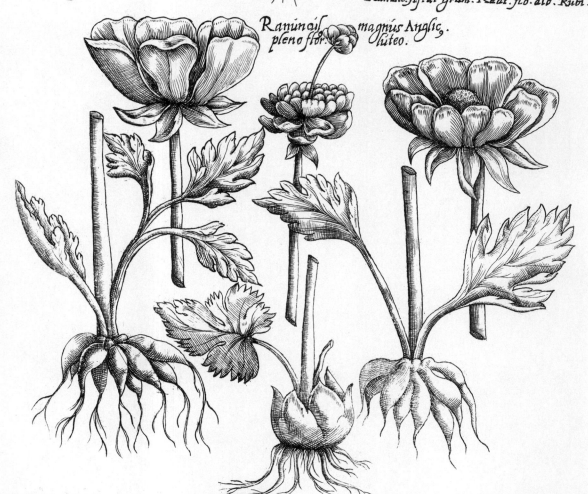

Caltha palustris pleno flo. aurea

Ranunculus Asiat: flo:flavo (crassioribꝰ) venis:

Ranun: pleno flore alba.

Ranun: glomerat. flore luteo.

Ranuncul⁹ hortensis luteo pleno flore ramosus

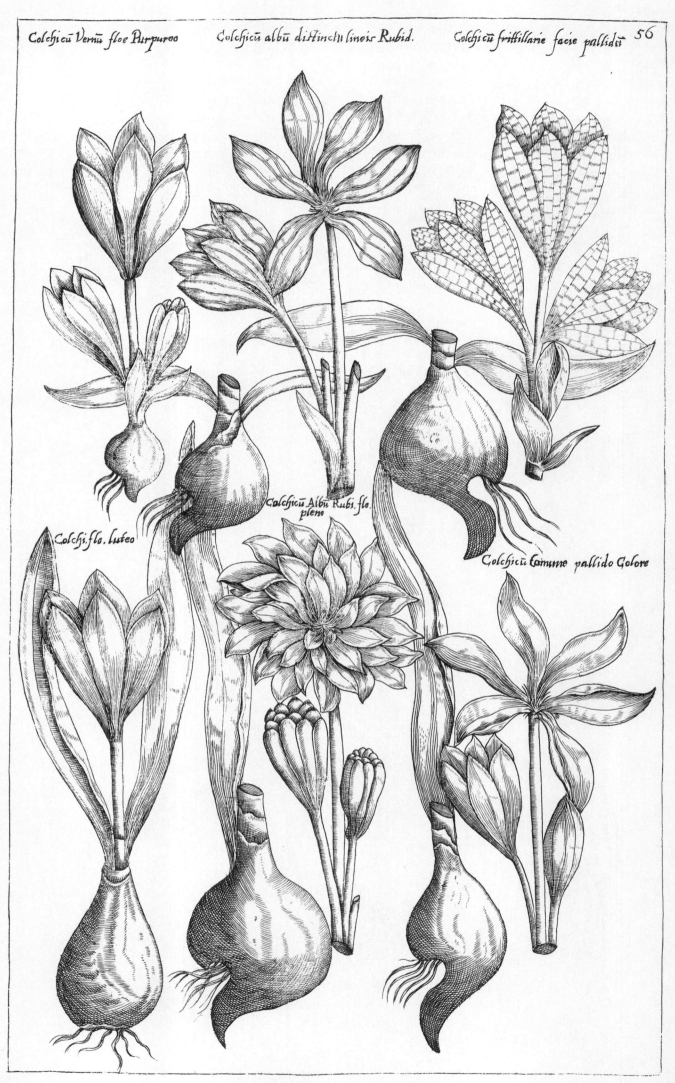

Colchicū Albū Rubi. flo.
pleno

Colchi. flo. luteo

Colchicū Comune pallido Colore

Ornithogalū Arabicū multi florū album
vmbilico Interiore nigro.

Ornithogalū Neapolitanū flor Intra Candidꝭ extra
cineraciꝭ.

Ornithogalon Luteum.

Ornithogalon Spicatum.

Ornithogalu Vni folij fl.b. albicante.

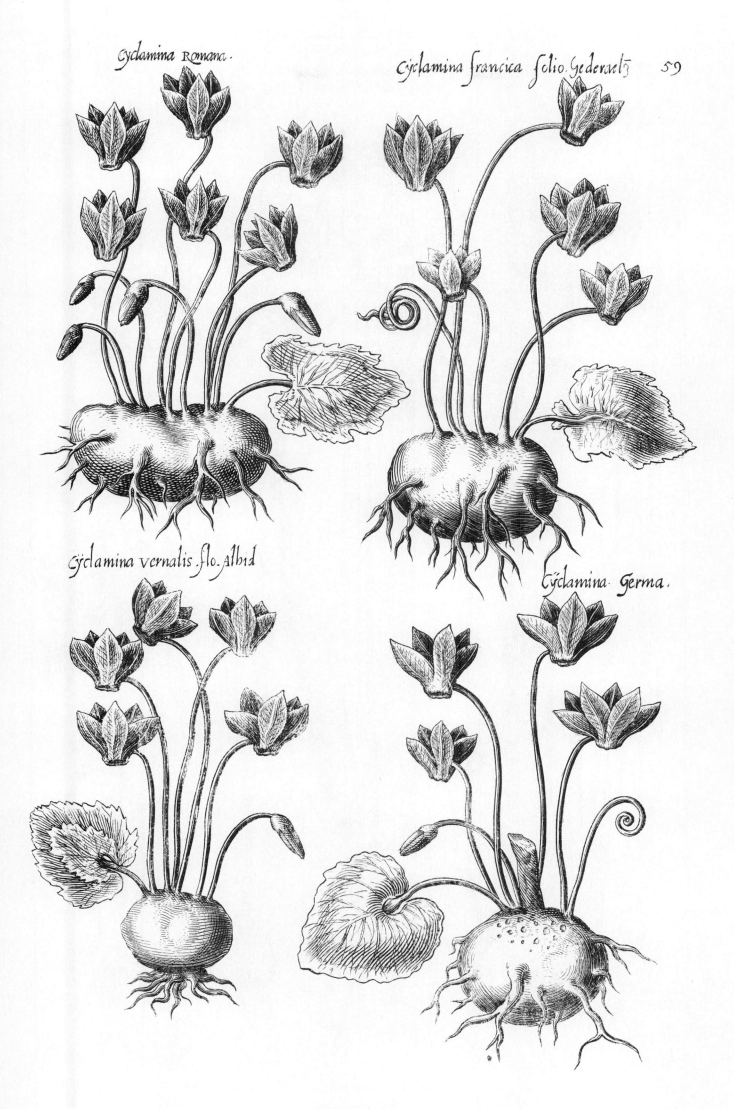

Cyclamina Romana.

Cyclamina francica folio. Gederxel3

Cyclamina vernalis. flo. Albid

Cyclamina. Germa.

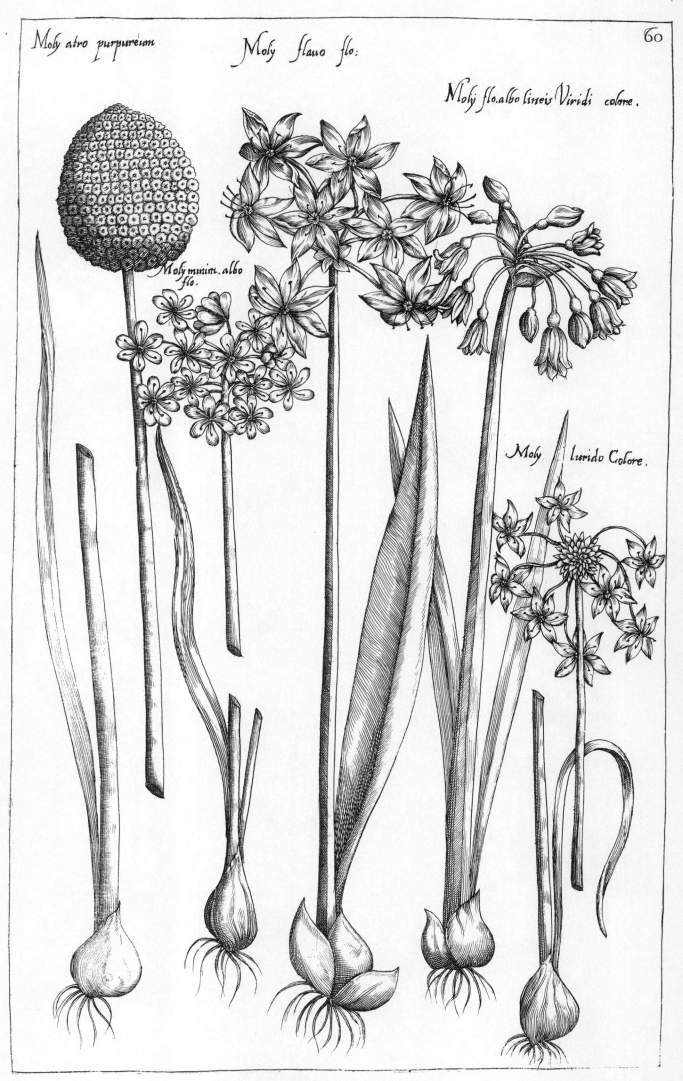

Moly atro purpureum

Moly flauo flo:

Moly flo. albo lineis Viridi colore.

Moly minim. albo
flo.

Moly lurido colore.

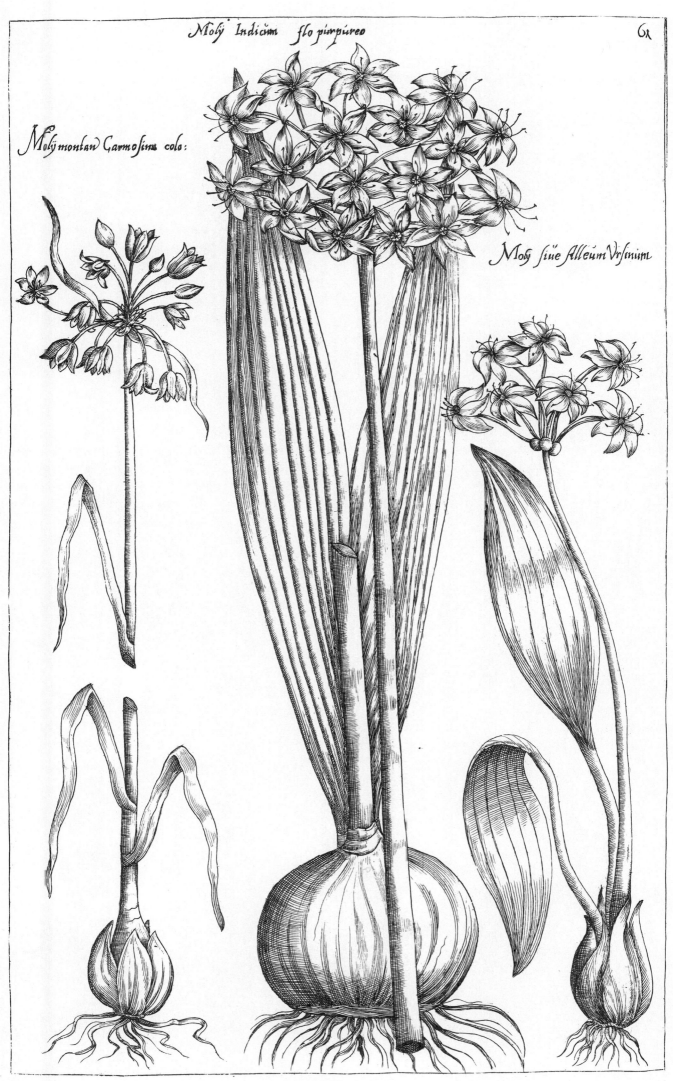

Moly Indicum flo purpureo

Moly montan Carmosino colo:

Moly siue Alleum Vrsinum

Moly montan Carmosino colo:

Sysirichium minus. *Sysirichium mas flore. cœruleo.* *Satyron e Guinea.*

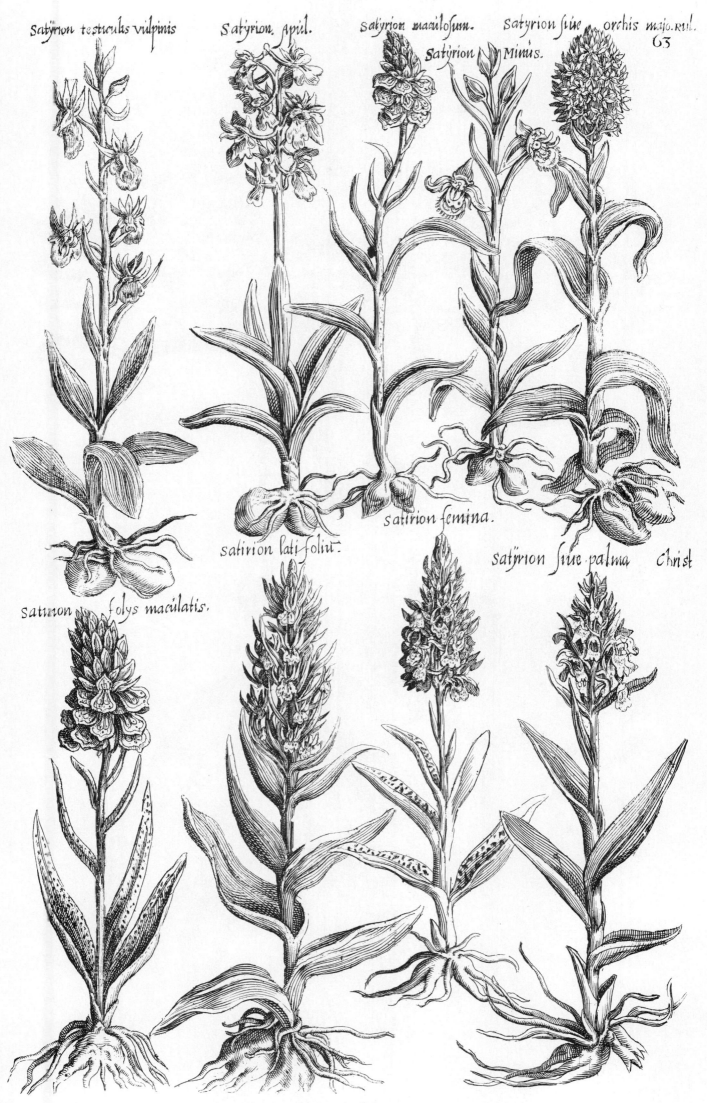

Satyrion testiculis vulpinis
Satyrion. April.
Satyrion maculosum.
Satyrion siue orchis maio. Rul.
Satyrion Minus.
satirion femina.
satirion lati foliu.
Satyrion siue palma Christ
satirion folys maculatis.

Pœonia multiplex Sanguinea.

Pœonia multiplex flore albicante.

Pœonia simplex alba.

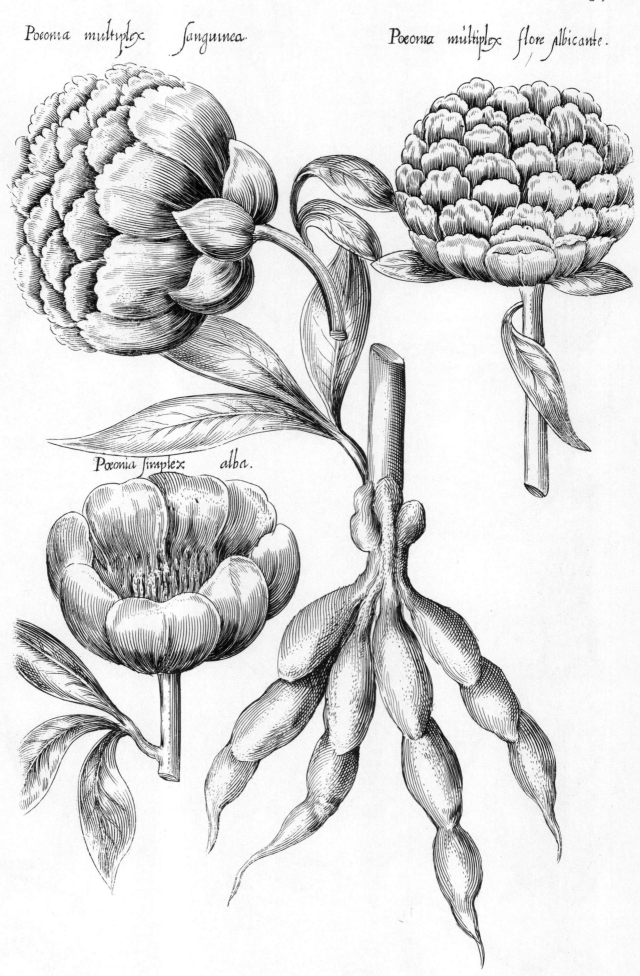

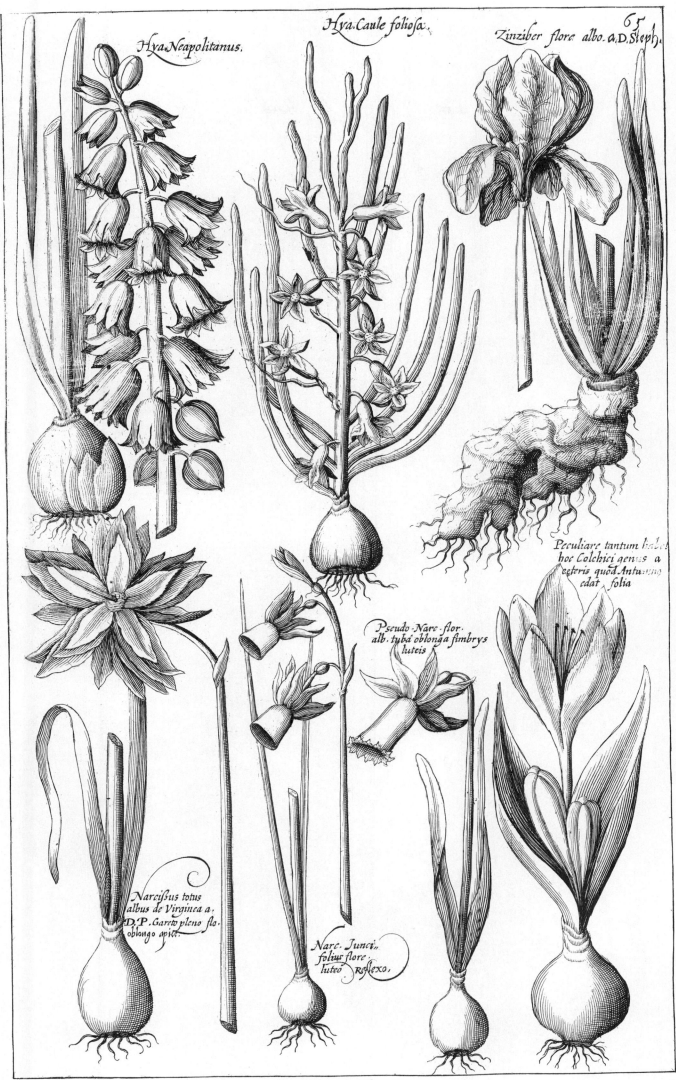

Hya. Neapolitanus.

Hya. Caule foliosa.

Zinziber flore albo. a. D. Steph.

Peculiare tantum habet
hoc Colchici genus a
ceteris quod Antumno
edat folia

Pseudo-Narc. flor.
alb. tuba oblonga fimbrys
luteis

Narcißus totus
albus de Virginea a.
D. P. Gareto pleno flo.
oblongo apice.

Narc. Junci„
folius flore
luteo Reflexo.

65 Miscellaneous Bulbous Plants.

Bulba opʃcũ rubra Promont. bonæ
Spẽ Tuteis Martagon. non diʃʃimilis
adhuc incognita.

Rodiæ bulbo.ˢᵃ.albā
Promont. bonæ ʃpei.collo
eximie craʃʃo

Gladiolus maximus
Promont. Bonæ ʃpei. flor. rubro in carnato

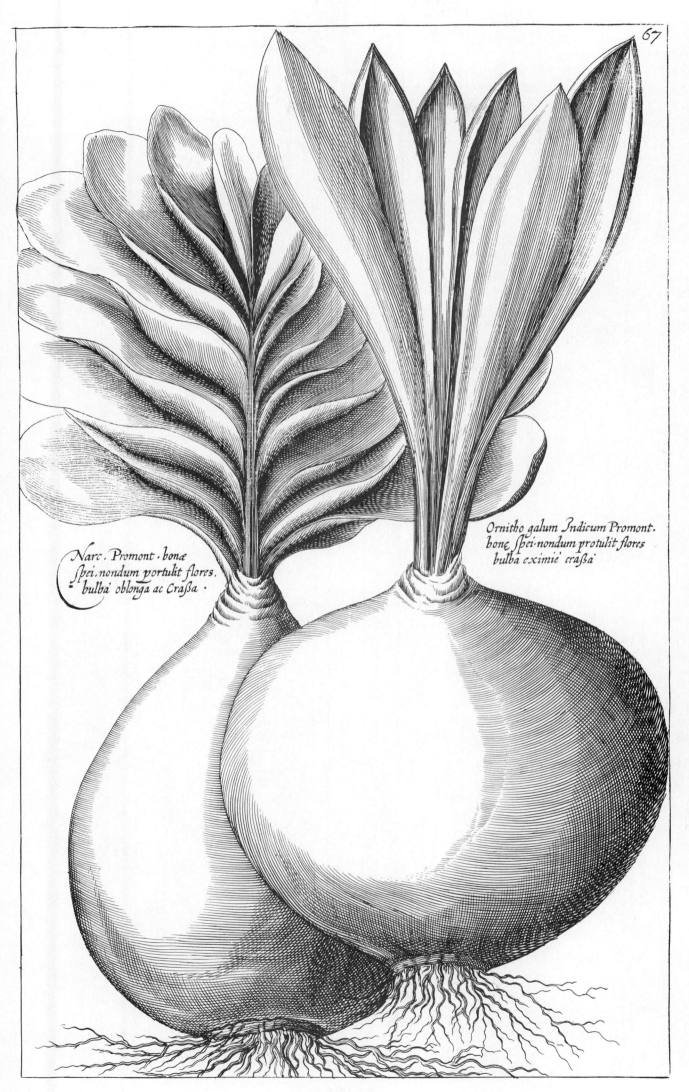

Narc. Promont. bonæ
spei. nondum portulit flores.
bulbà oblonga ac Craßa .

Ornitho galum Indicum Promont.
bonę spei. nondum protulit flores
bulba eximie craßa

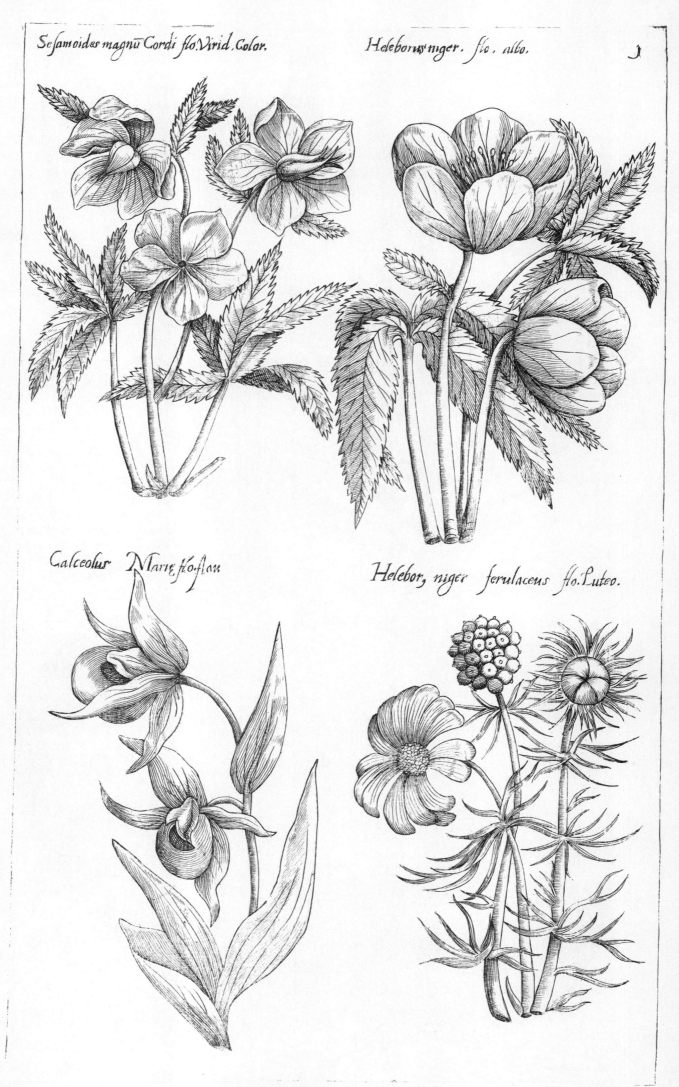

Sesamoides magnū Cordi flo. Virid. Color.

Heleborus niger. flo. albo.

Calceolus Mariæ flo. flau.

Helebor, niger ferulaceus flo. Luteo.

II-1 Hellebores and Others.

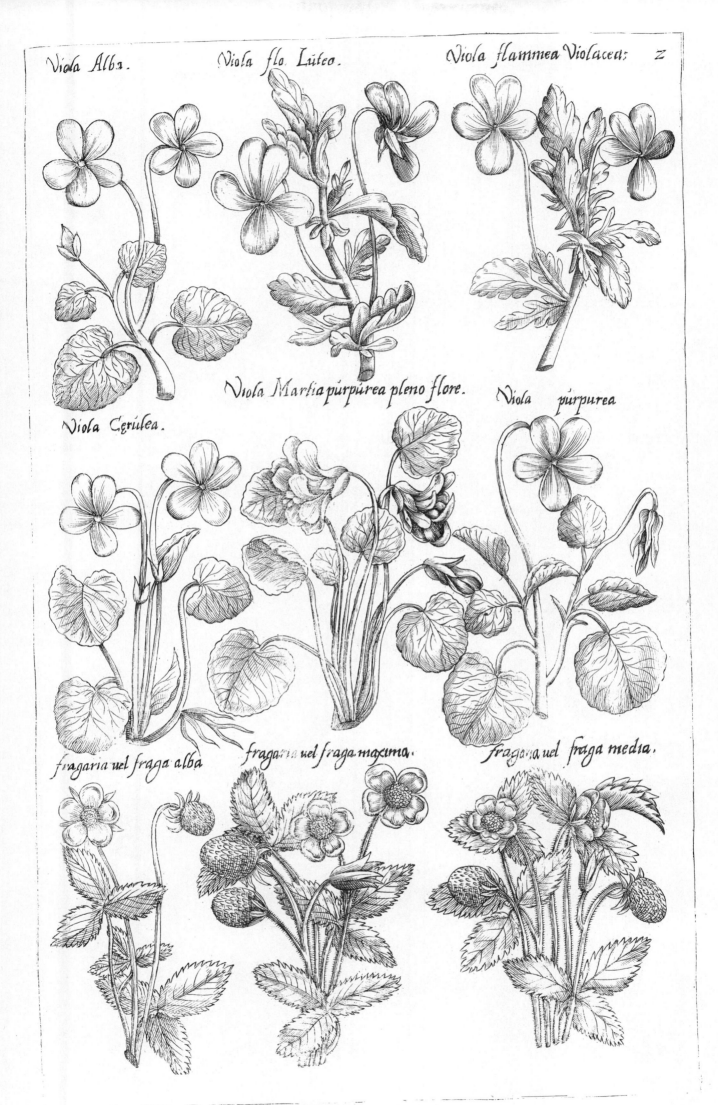

Viola Alba.

Viola flo. Luteo.

Viola flammea Violacea:

Viola Martia purpurea pleno flore.

Viola purpurea

Viola Cerulea.

fragaria uel fraga alba

fragaria uel fraga maxima.

fragaria uel fraga media.

II-2 Pansies, Violets and Strawberries.

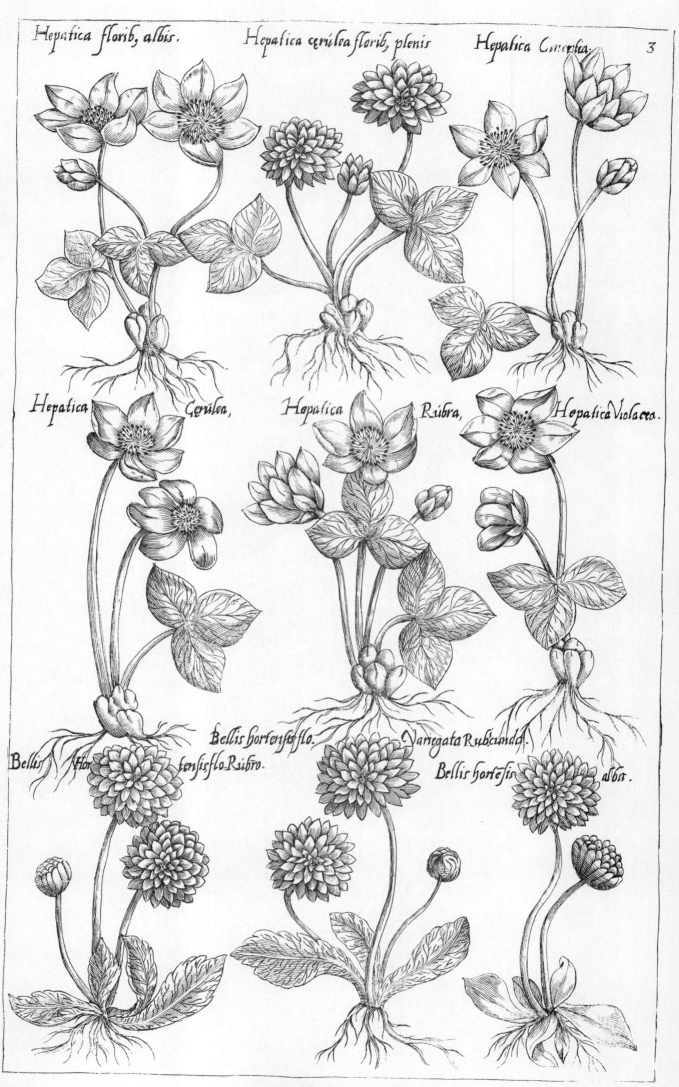

Hepatica florib, albis. Hepatica cerulea florib, plenis. Hepatica Cinerea.

Hepatica   Cerulea,   Hepatica   Rubra,   Hepatica Violacea.

Bellis   Flor-   Bellis hortensis flo.   Variegata Rubcunda.
tensis flo. Rubro.   Bellis hortensis   albis.

II-3   Hepatica and Bellis.

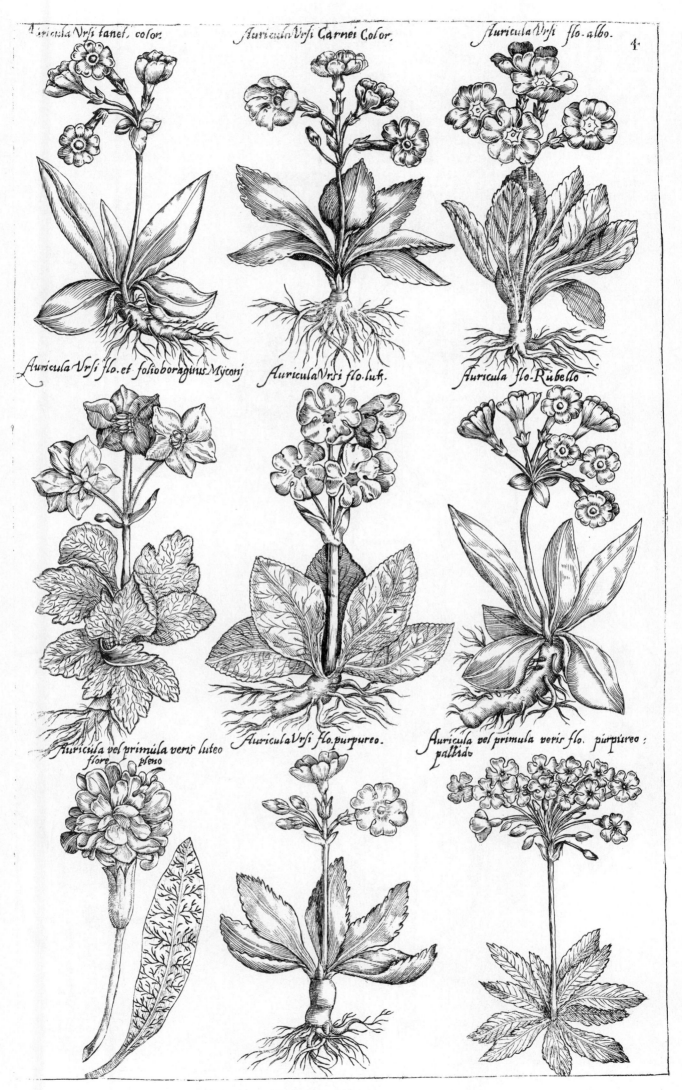

Auricula Vrsi tanet, color.   Auricula Vrsi Carnei Color.   Auricula Vrsi flo. albo.   4.

Auricula Vrsi flo. et folio boraginis Myconj   Auricula Vrsi flo. luk.   Auricula flo. Rubello.

Auricula vel primula veris luteo flore pleno   Auricula Vrsi flo. purpureo.   Auricula vel primula veris flo. purpureo pallido

II-4   Primroses and Others.

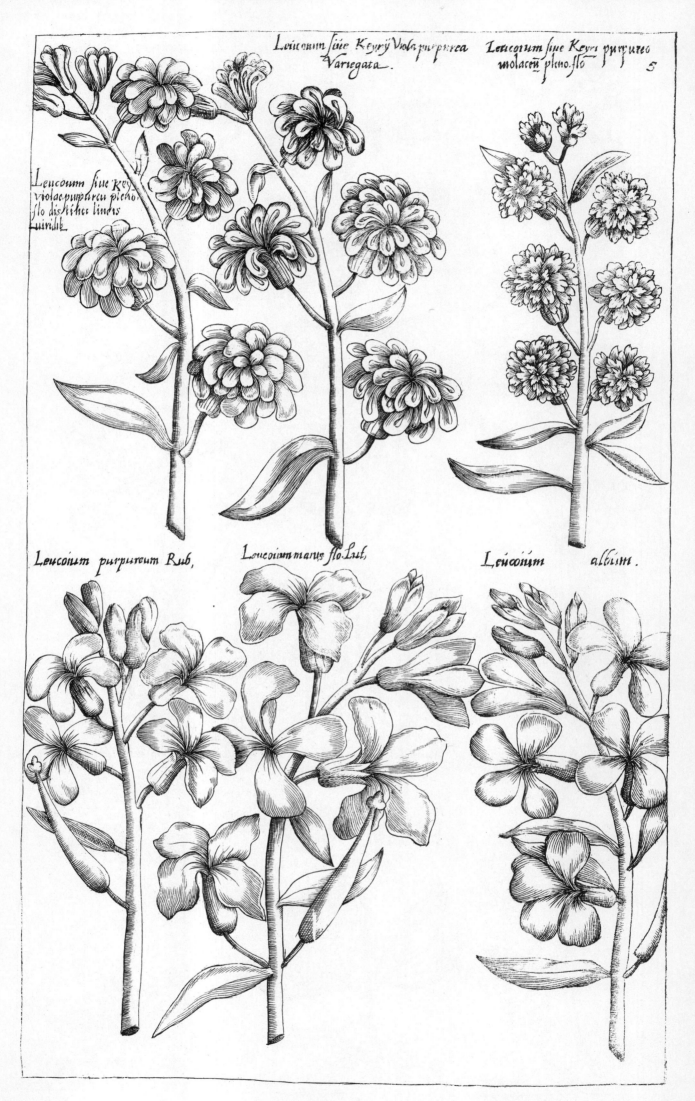

Leucoium siue Keyri Viola purpurea
Variegata.

Leucoium siue Keyri purpureo
violaceu pleno flo
5

Leucoium siue Keyri
violae purpureu plenō
flo dis tinct lineis
viridis

Leucoium purpureum Rub,

Leucoium marus flo Lut,

Leucoium album.

II-5 Stocks.

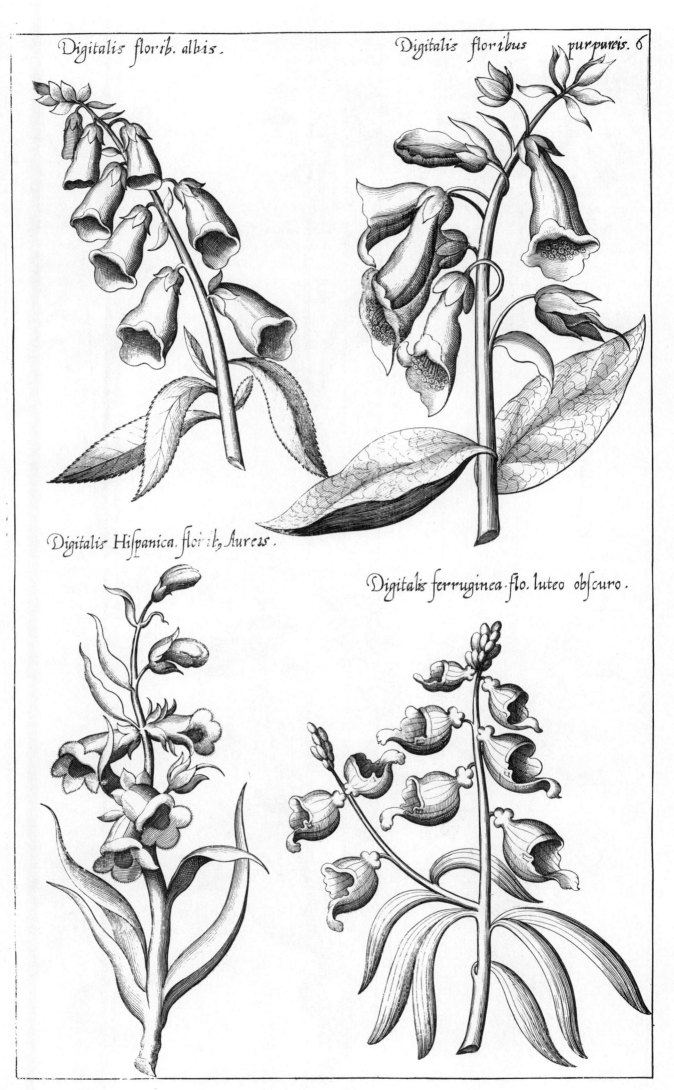

Digitalis florib. albis.

Digitalis floribus purpureis. 6

Digitalis Hispanica. florib, Aureis.

Digitalis ferruginea. flo. luteo obscuro.

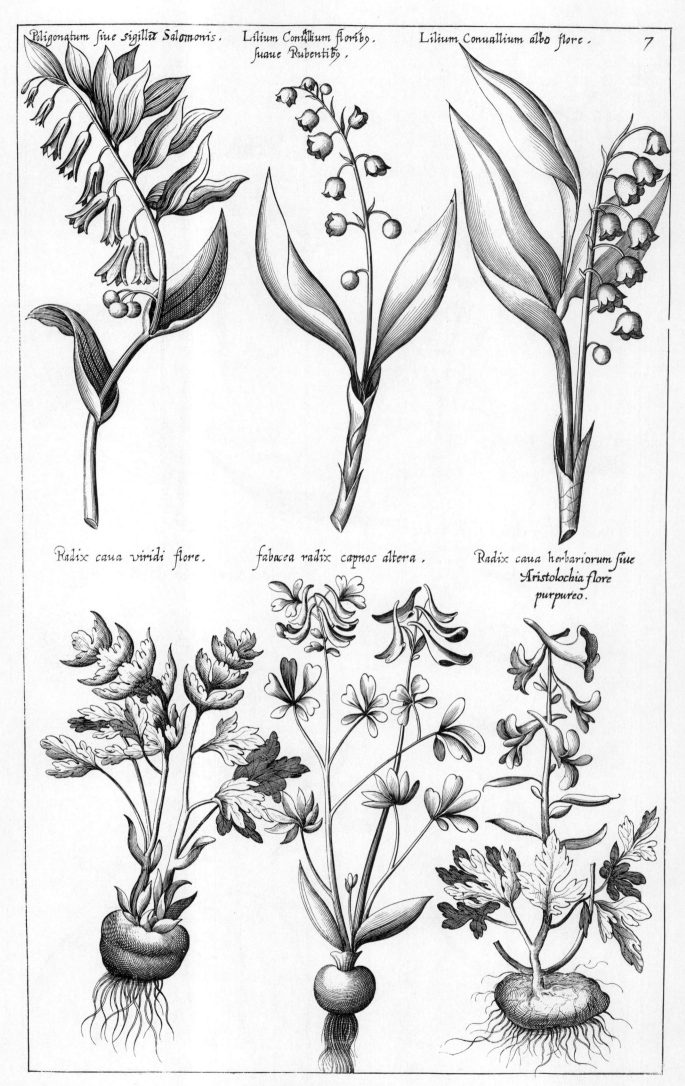

Poligonatum siue sigilla Salomonis.   Lilium Conuallium floribs.   Lilium Conuallium albo flore.
                                         suaue Rubentibs.

Radix caua viridi flore.   fabacea radix capnos altera.   Radix caua herbariorum siue
                                          Aristolochia flore
                                           purpureo.

II-7 Varied Plants.

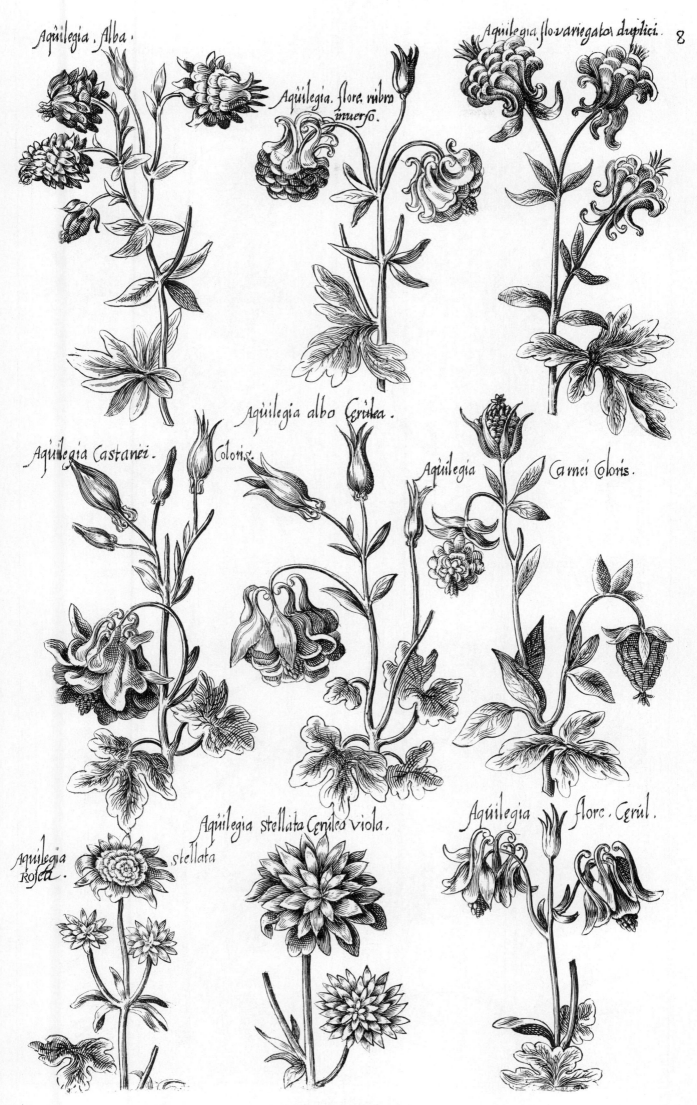

Aquilegia. Alba.

Aquilegia. flore. rubro inuerso.

Aquilegia flo variegato duplici.

Aquilegia albo Cerulea.

Aquilegia Castanei. Coloris.

Aquilegia Carnei Coloris.

Aquilegia stellata Cerulea viola.

Aquilegia Roseta.

stellata

Aquilegia flore. Cerul.

II-8   Columbines.

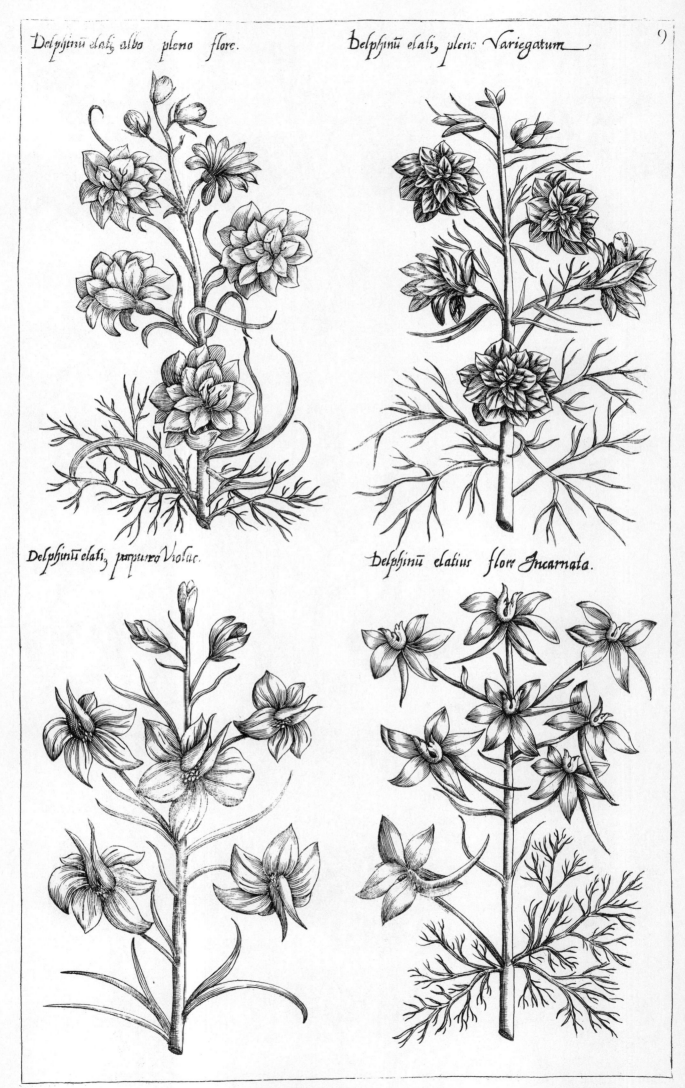

Delphinū elatis albo pleno flore.

Delphinū elatis pleno Variegatum

Delphinū elatis purpureo Violac.

Delphinū elatius flore Incarnata.

II-9 Delphiniums.

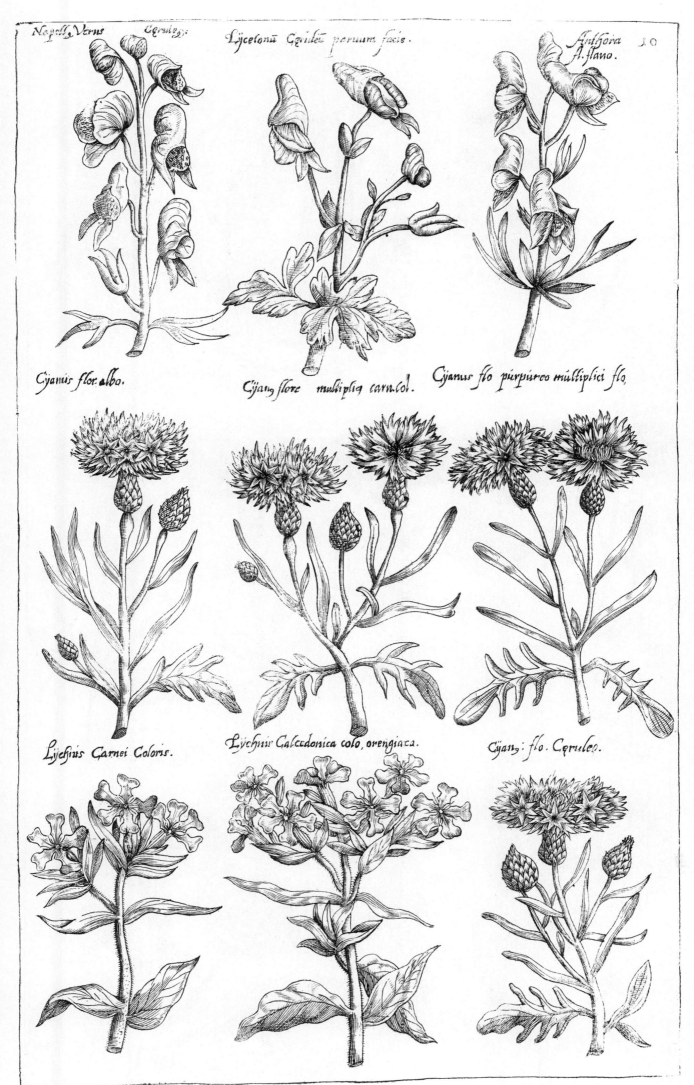

Napell. Verus Cærule.   Lycetonū Cærūleū peruum facie.   Anthora A. flauo.

Cyanus flor. alba.   Cyanꝰ flore multipliq carn.col.   Cyanus flo purpureo multiplici flo.

Lychnis Carnei Coloris.   Lychnis Calcedonica colo, orengiaca.   Cyanꝰ: flo. Cæruleo.

II-10   Various Plants.

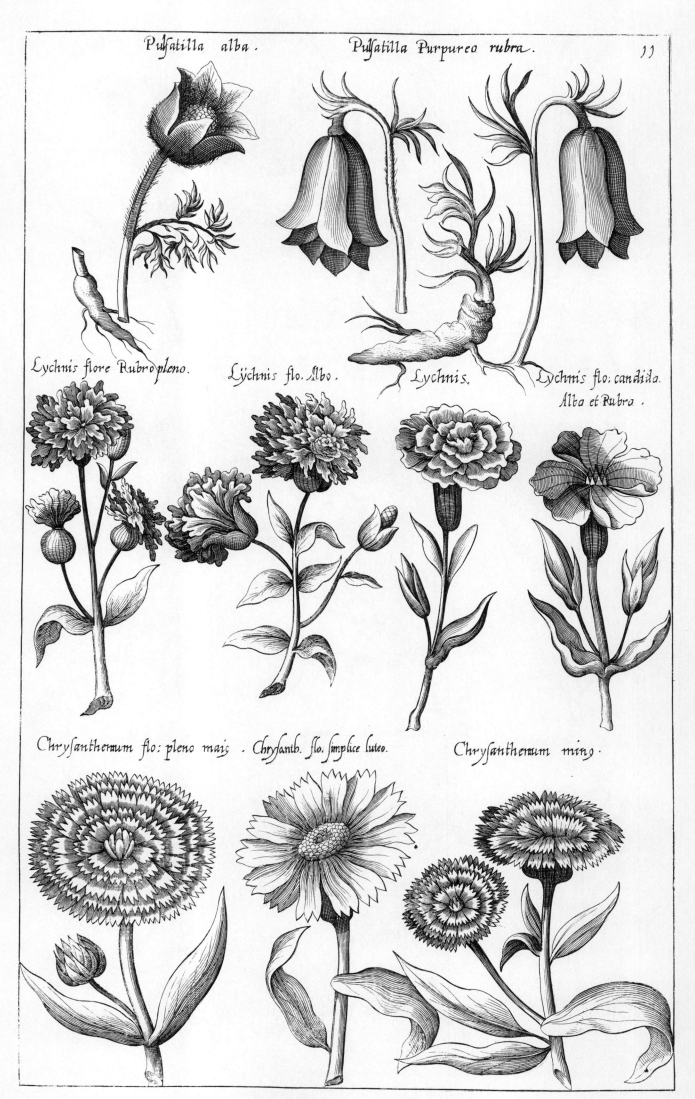

Pusatilla alba.   Pusatilla Purpureo rubra.

Lychnis flore Rubro pleno.   Lychnis flo. Albo.   Lychnis.   Lychnis flo: candida.
Alba et Rubro.

Chrysanthemum flo: pleno mais.   Chrysanth. flo. simplice luteo.   Chrysanthemum mins.

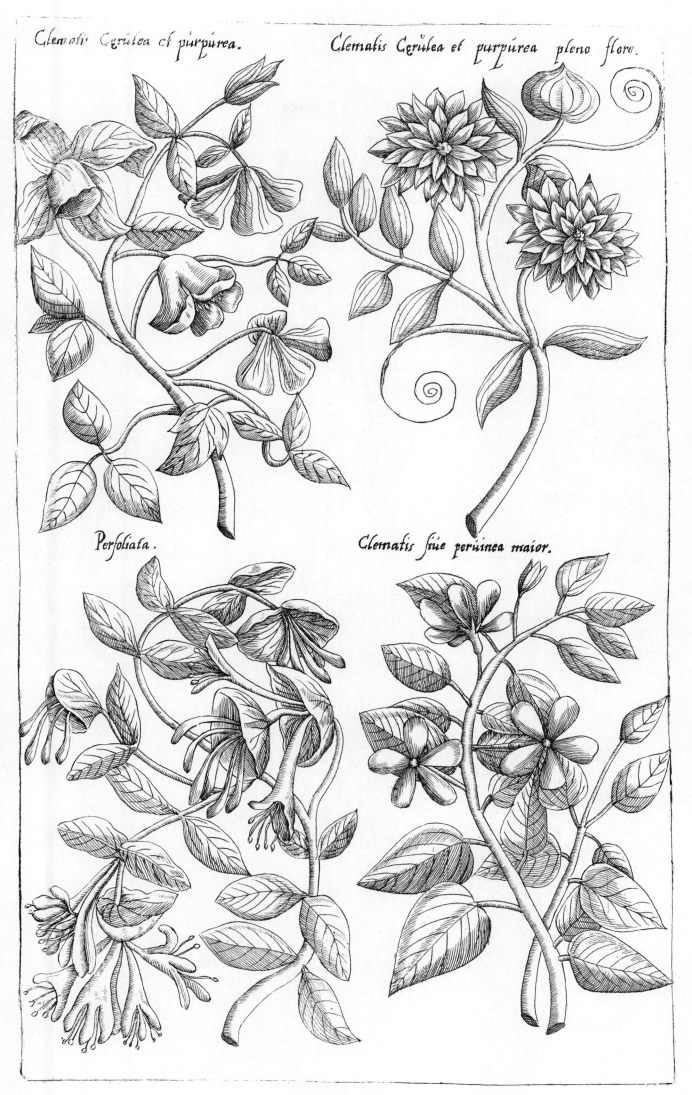

Clematis Cærulea et purpurea.

Clematis Cærulea et purpurea pleno floro.

Perfoliata.

Clematis siue peruinca maior.

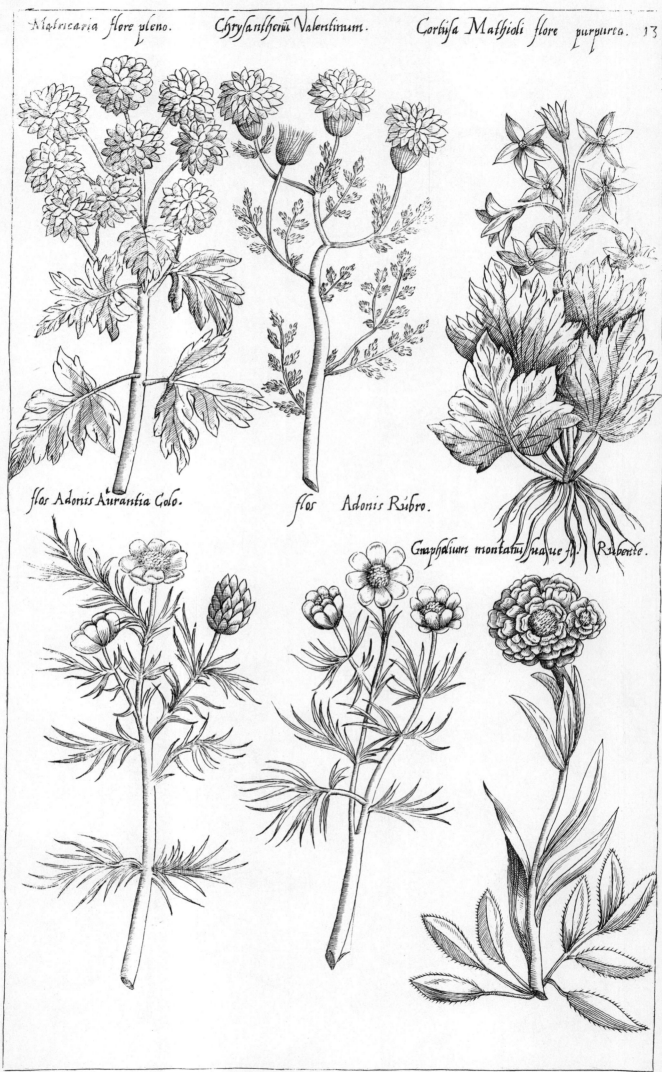

flos Adonis Aurantia Colo.   flos   Adonis Rubro.

Gnaphalium montanu suaue fl. Rubente.

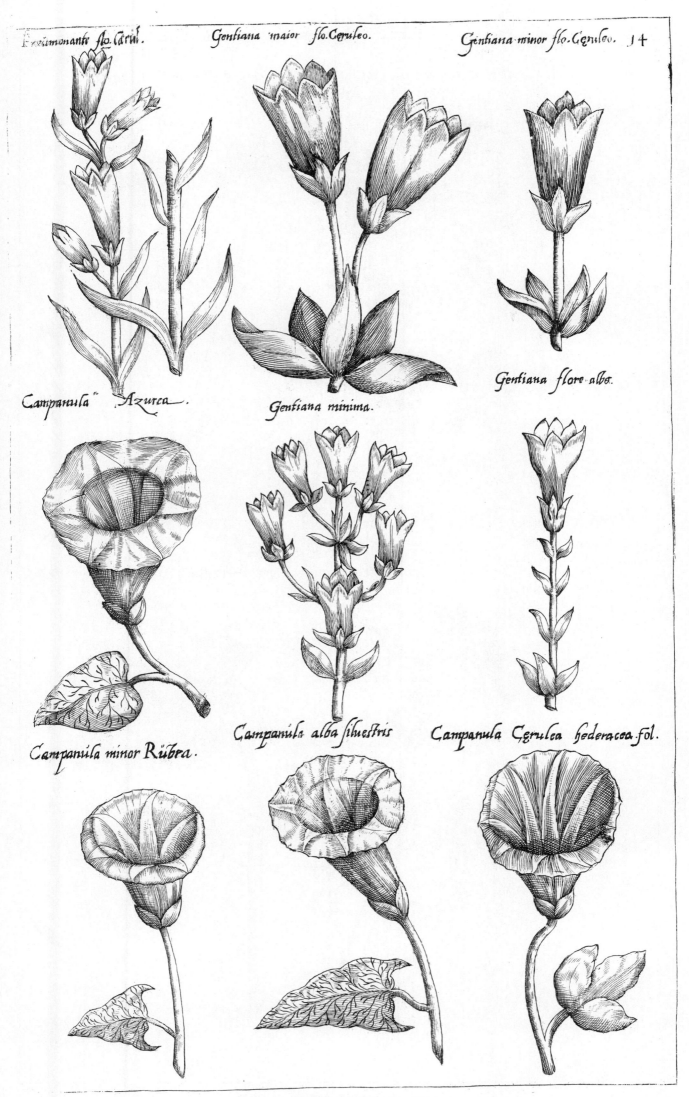

Fccumonante flo. Cærul. Gentiana maior flo. Cæruleo. Gentiana minor flo. Cæruleo. 14

Campanula Azurea. Gentiana minima. Gentiana flore albo.

Campanula minor Rubra. Campanula alba filuestris Campanula Cerulea hederacea fol.

II-14 Gentians and Morning-Glories.

Melanthium flo. multiplici.   Melanthium vulgare.

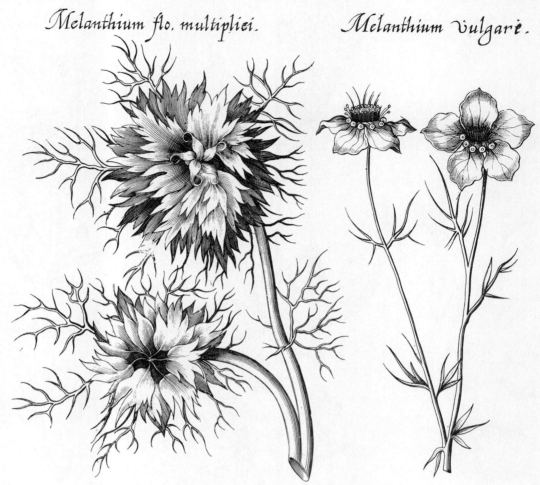

Melanthium Hispanicum Amplo. flo.

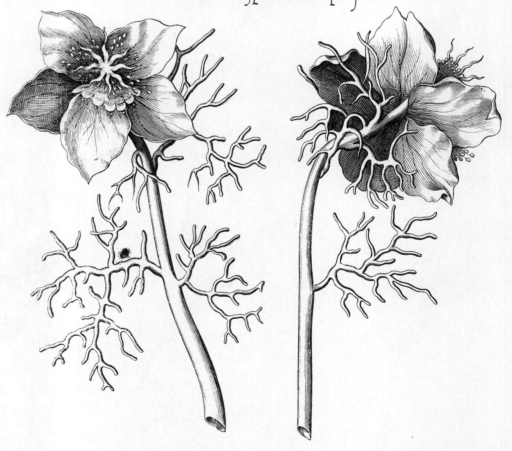

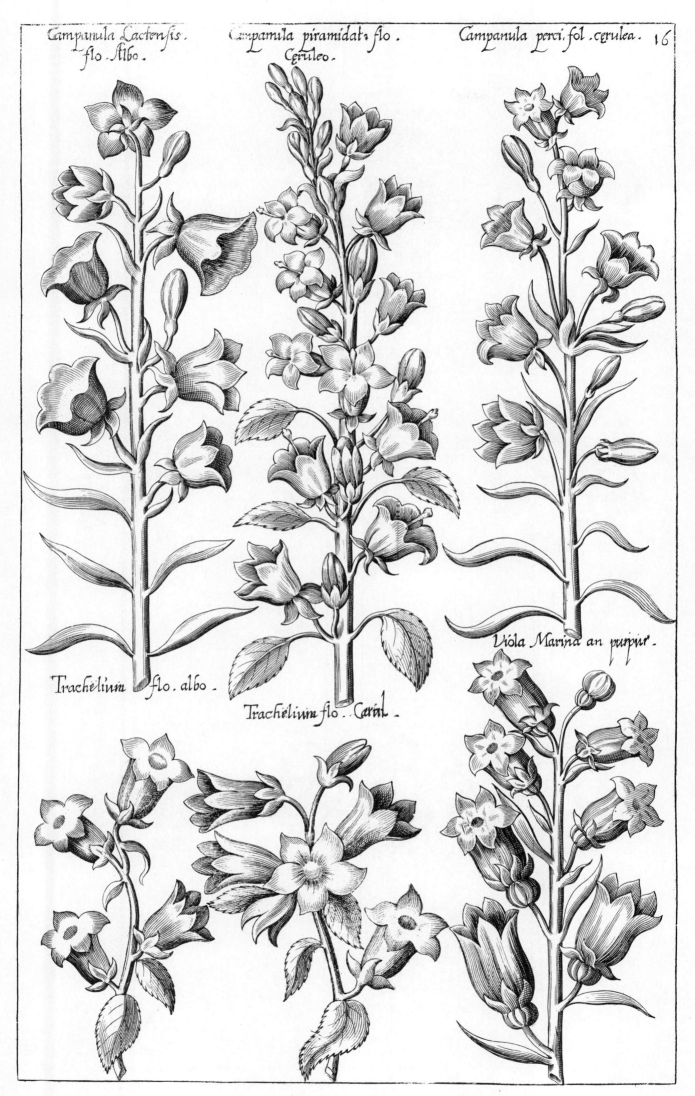

Campanula Lactensis. flo. Albo.

Campanula piramidal. flo. Ceruleo.

Campanula perci. fol. cerulea.

Trachelium flo. albo.

Trachelium flo. Ceril.

Viola Marina an purpur.

Cariophyllus albus totus et
noïulis Rubris distinctâ.

Cariphyllo alb. flammulis P. u.
berruïz.

Cariophyllo albus   lineis 17
rubris subtilissime distincïis.

Cariophyllus totus albus

Cariophyllus.   In,,
curnata

Cariophyllus purpureo   punctulis
purpurei coloris.

Cariophyllo sub uiridi
flore.

Cariophyll Rubens.

Cariphyll alba.... lineis
Cramosinii coloris.

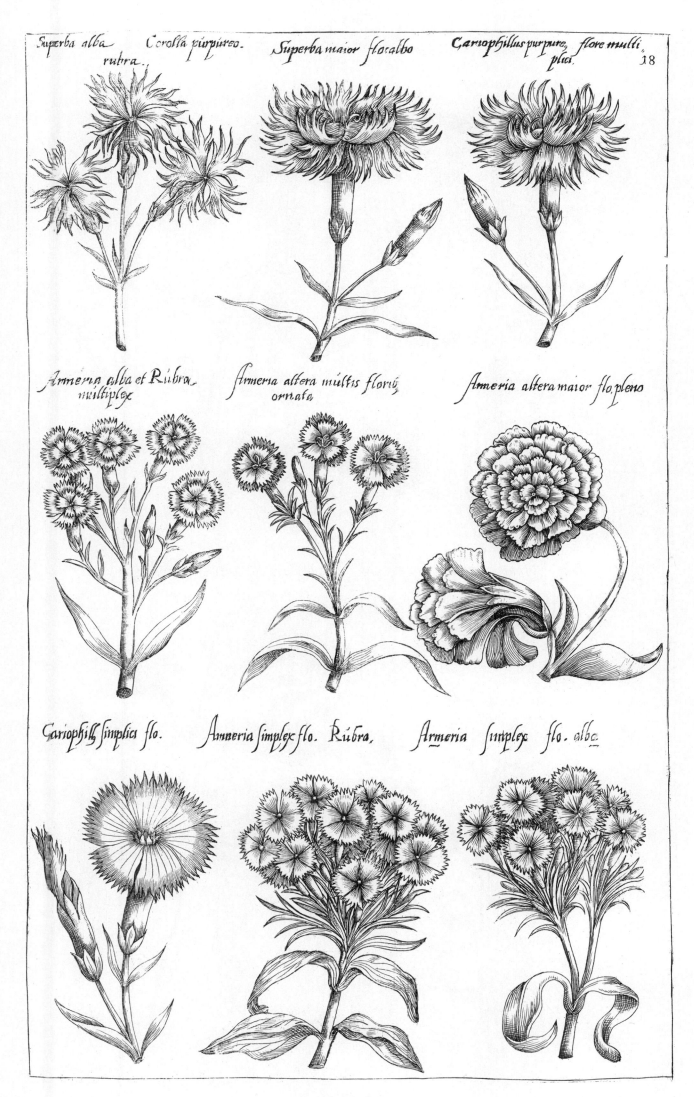

Superba alba   Corolla purpureo.   Superba maior floralbo   Cariophillus purpure, flore multi plici.

Armeria alba et Rubra multiplex   Armeria altera multis floriis ornata   Ameria altera maior flo. pleno

Cariophill simplici flo.   Ameria simplex flo. Rubra.   Armeria simplex flo. alba

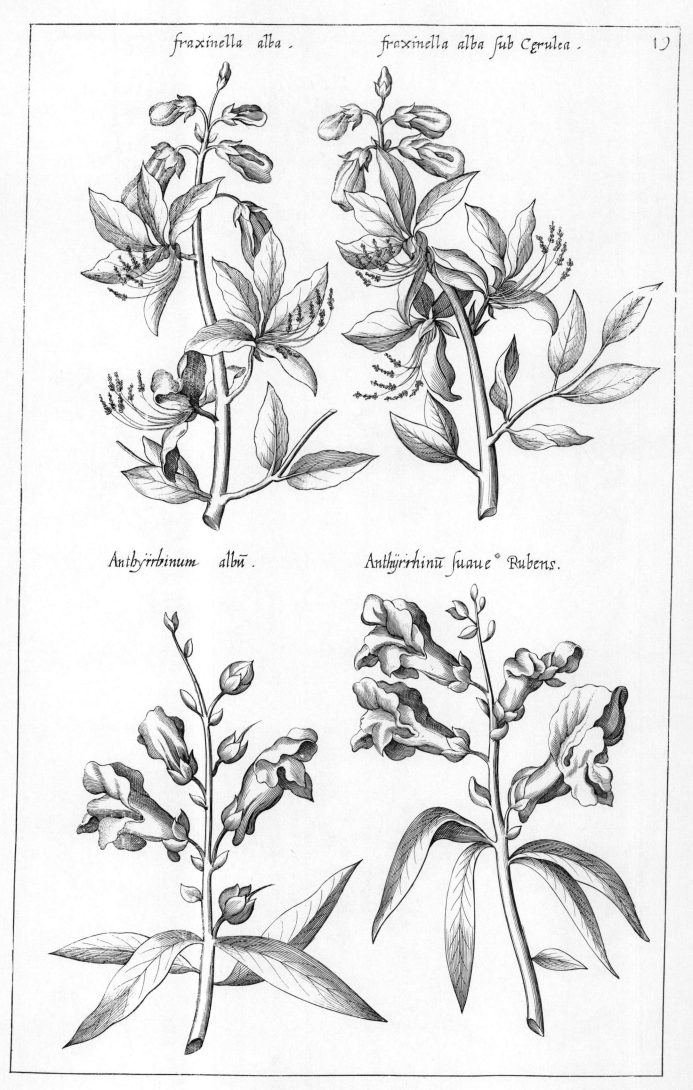

fraxinella alba.   *fraxinella alba sub Cærulea.*

Anthyrrbinum albū.   *Anthÿrrhinū suaue° Rubens.*

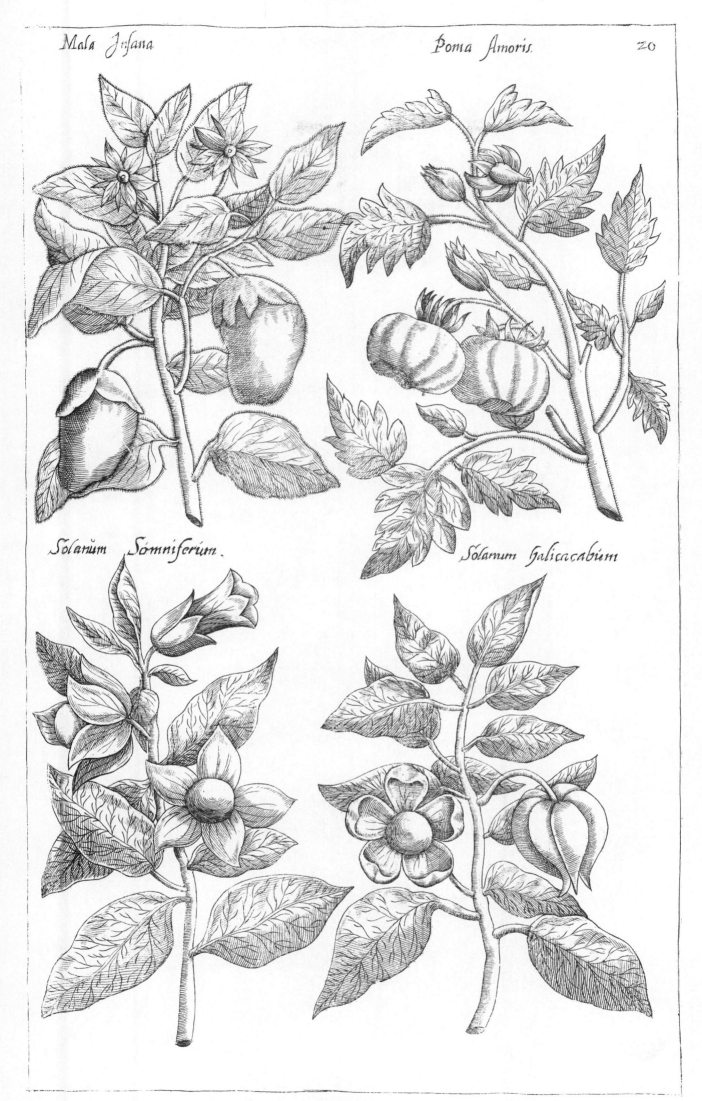

Mala Jnfana

Poma Amoris.

Solanum Somniferum.

Solanum Halicacabum

II-20   Economic Solanids.

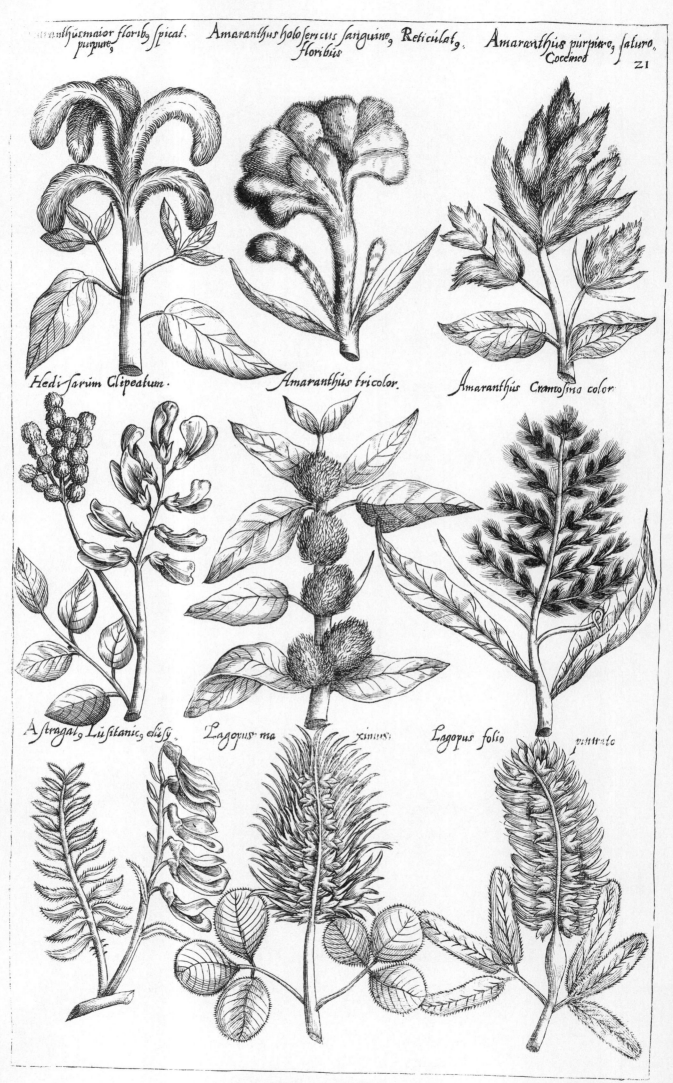

Amaranthus maior florib, spicat. purpure,   Amaranthus holosericus sanguine, Reticulat, floribus   Amaranthus purpureo saturo, Coccineo

Z1

Hedisarum Clipeatum.   Amaranthus tricolor.   Amaranthus Cramosino color.

Astragal, Lusitanic, elisy   Lagopus maximus   Lagopus folio pinnato

II-21 Various Plants.

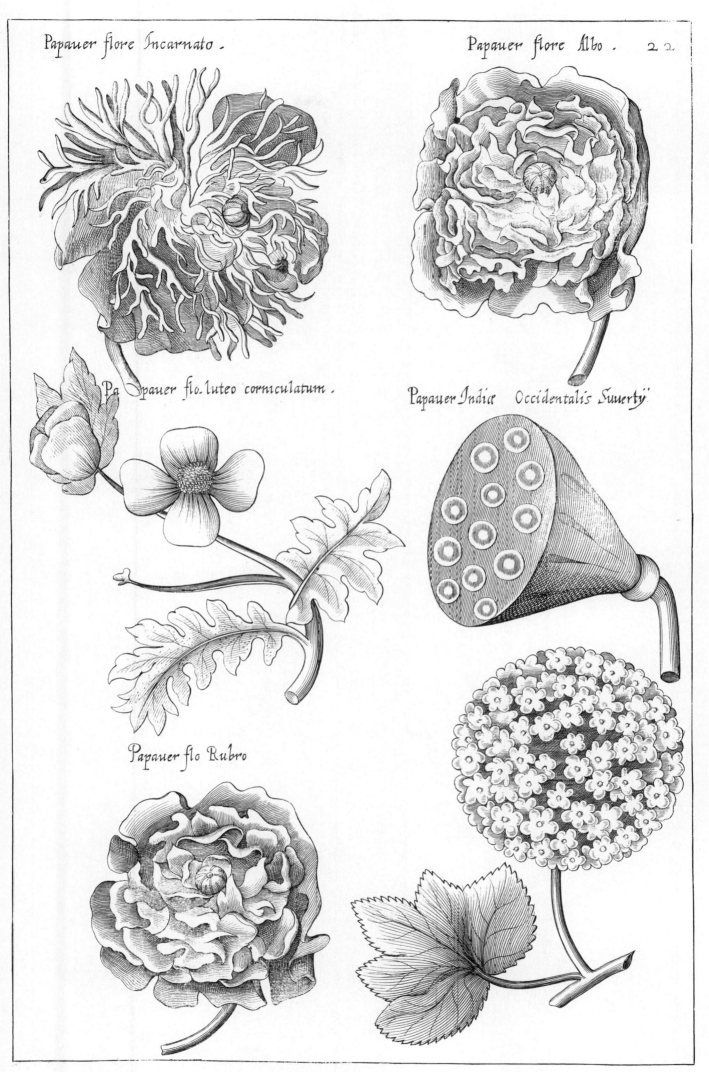

Papauer flore Incarnato.

Papauer flore Albo.

22

Pa Spauer flo. luteo corniculatum.

Papauer Indiæ Occidentalis Suuertÿ

Papauer flo Rubro

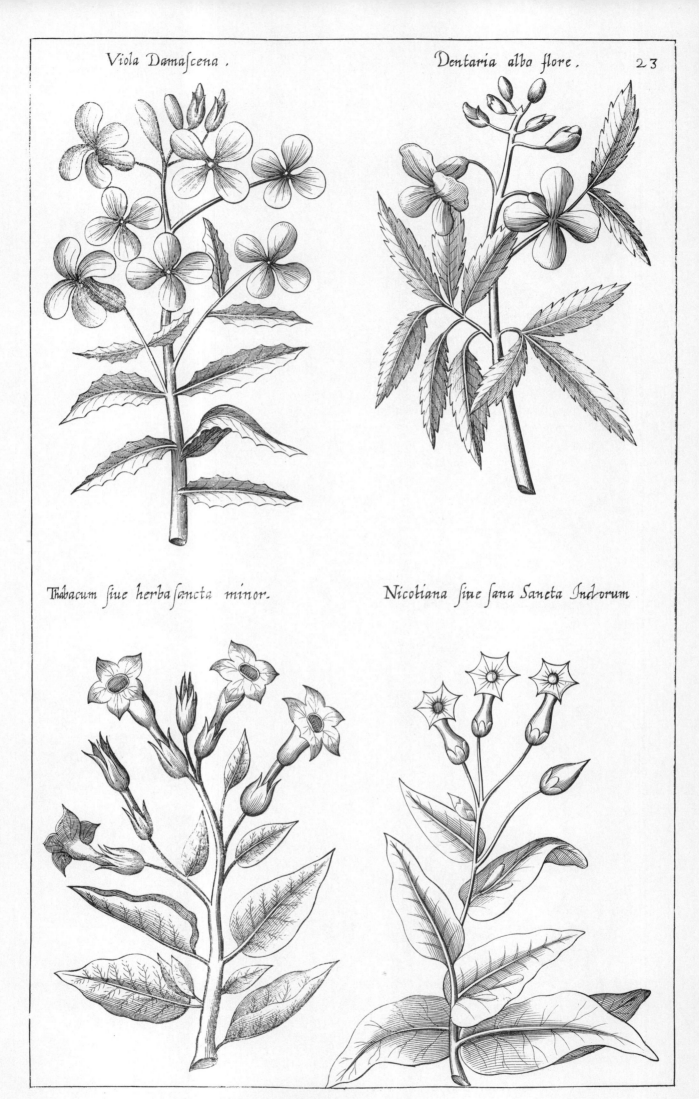

Viola Damaſcena.

Dentaria alba flore.

Thabacum ſiue herba ſancta minor.

Nicotiana ſiue ſana Sancta Indorum.

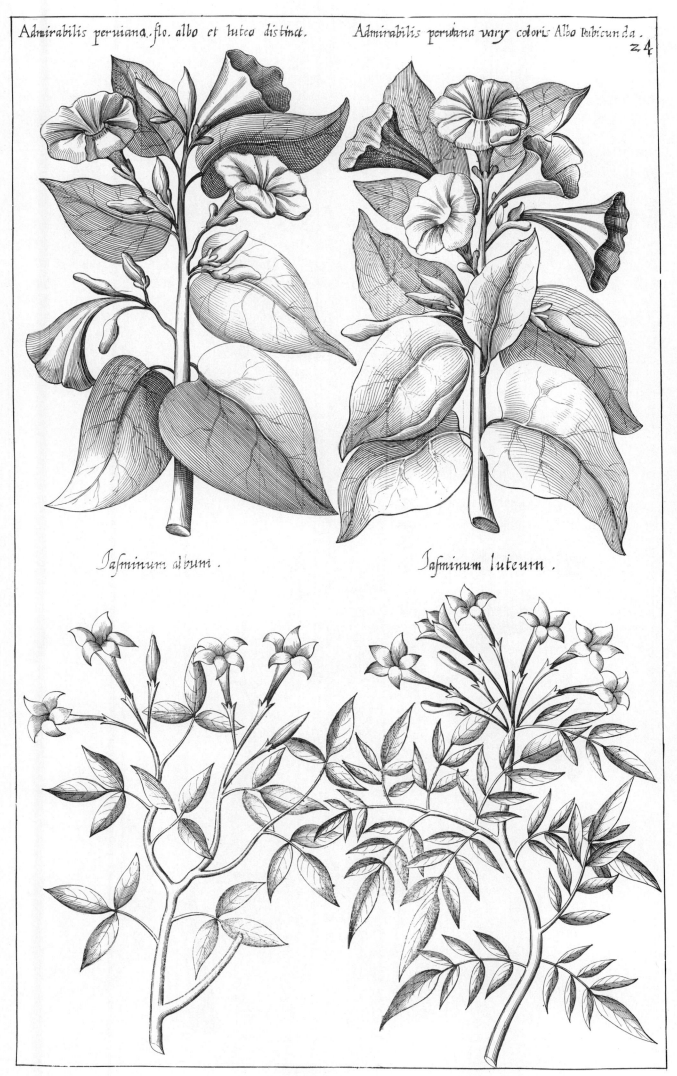

Jasminum album.   Jasminum luteum.

Solis flos Peruuianus.   *Solis flos minor.*

II-25   Sunflowers.

Aphricanus flos maximus pleno flore Aurantio.
Colore.

Aphricang flos maximus simplex flo. luteo.

26

Aphricanus flos simplex.

Aphricanus flos alter pleno flore.

Aphricanus maior flo. pleno.

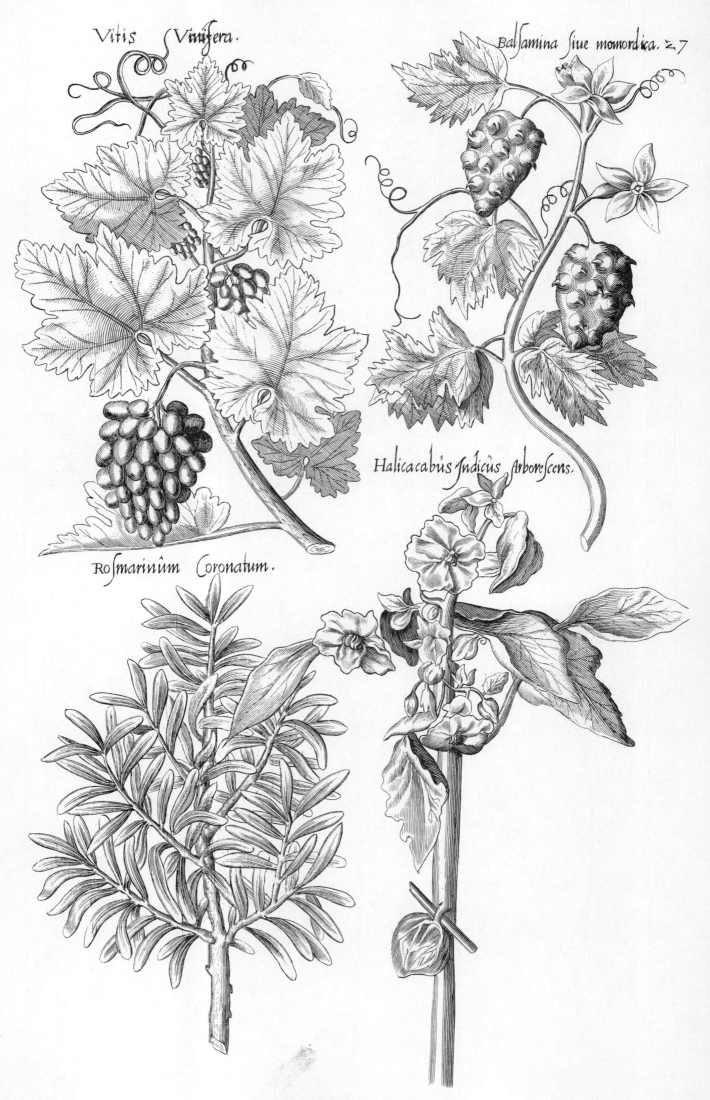

Vitis Vinifera.

Balsamina siue momordica. 27

Halicacabus Indicus Arborescens.

Rosmarinum Coronatum.

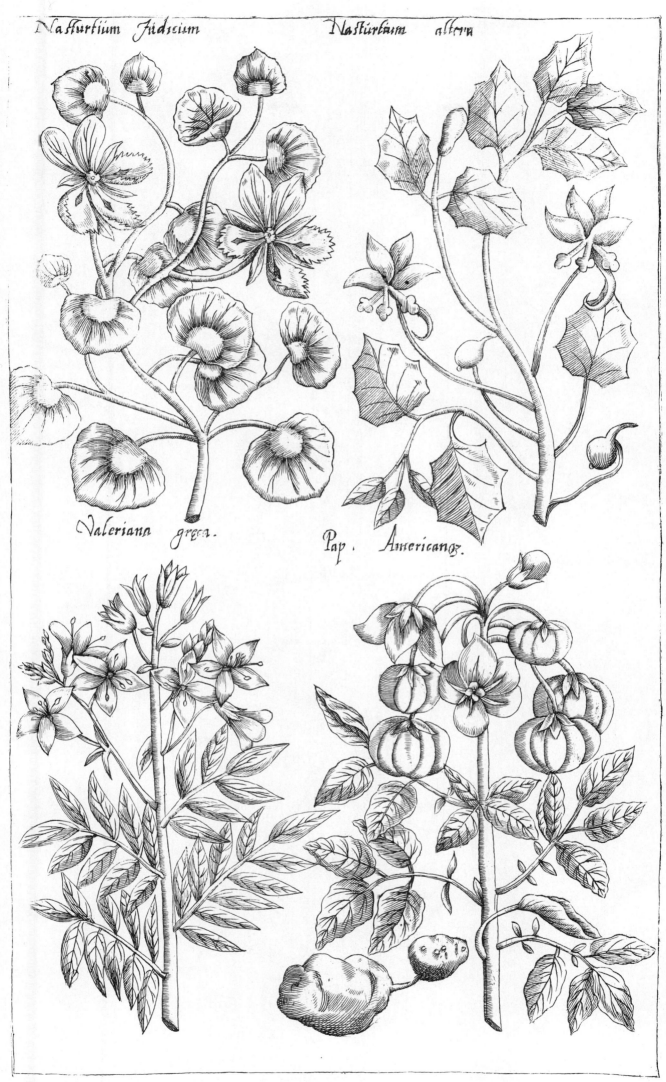

Nasturtium Judaicum

Nasturtium altera

Valeriana greca.

Pap. Americanæ.

II-28   Various Plants.

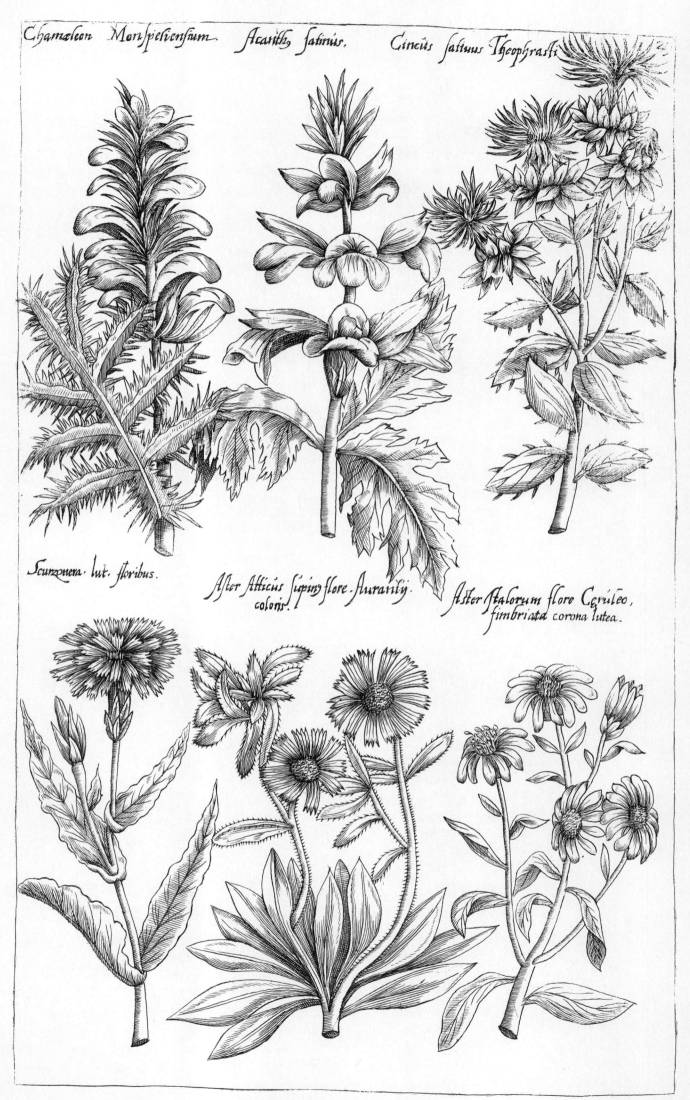

Chamæleon Monspeliensium.   Acanth. satiuus.   Cineus satiuus Theophrasti

Scurzonera. lut. floribus.

Aster Atticus supiny flore Aurantij. coloris.

Aster stalorum flore Cæruleo, fimbriata corona lutea.

II-29   Various Plants.

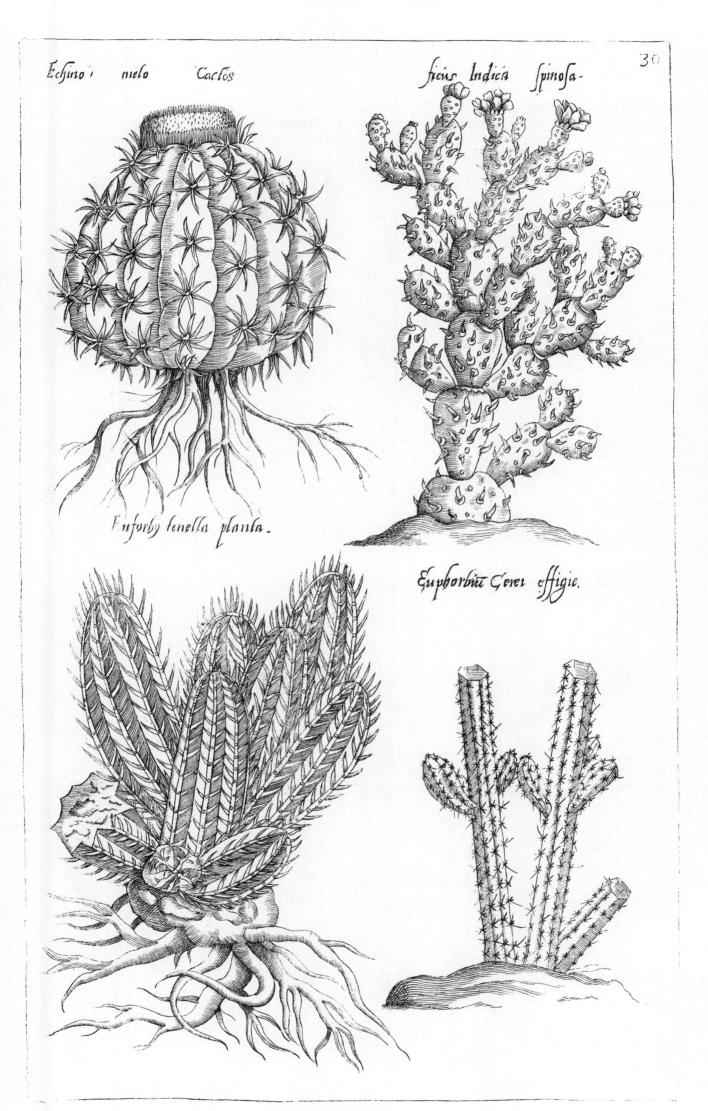

Echino ; melo   Cactos   ficus Indica spinofa.

Euforby tenella planta.

Euphorbiu Cerei effigie.

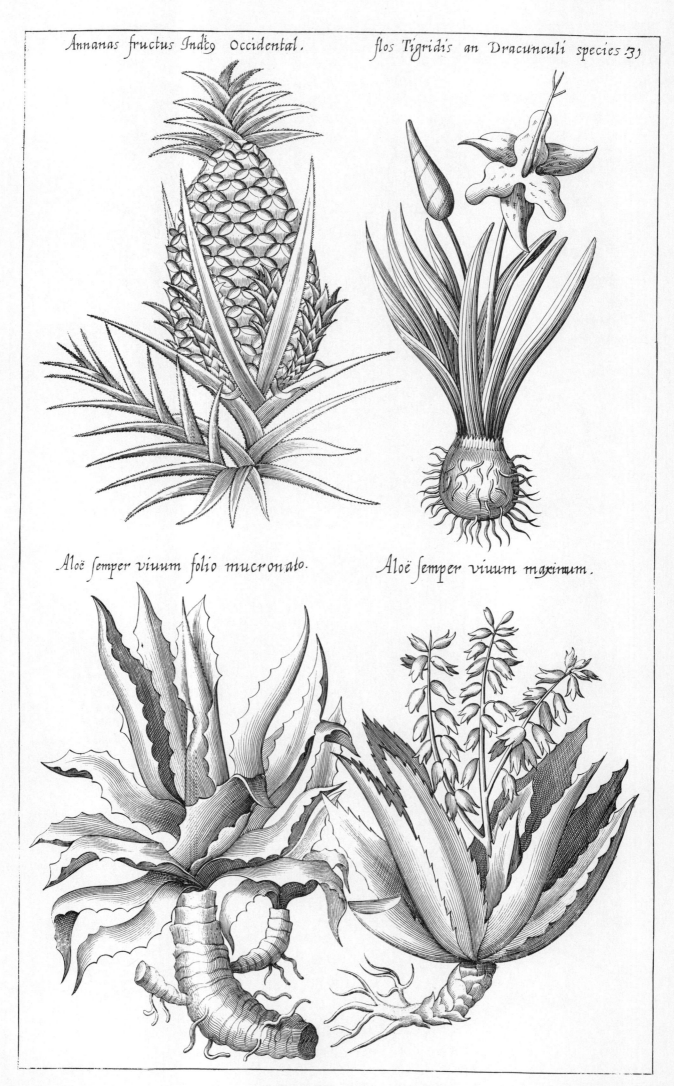

Annanas fructus Indię Occidental.

flos Tigridis an Dracunculi species 31

Aloë semper viuum folio mucronato.

Aloë semper viuum maximum.

Canna Indica, flore Luteo.   Canna Indica flore Rubro.

II-32 Cannas.

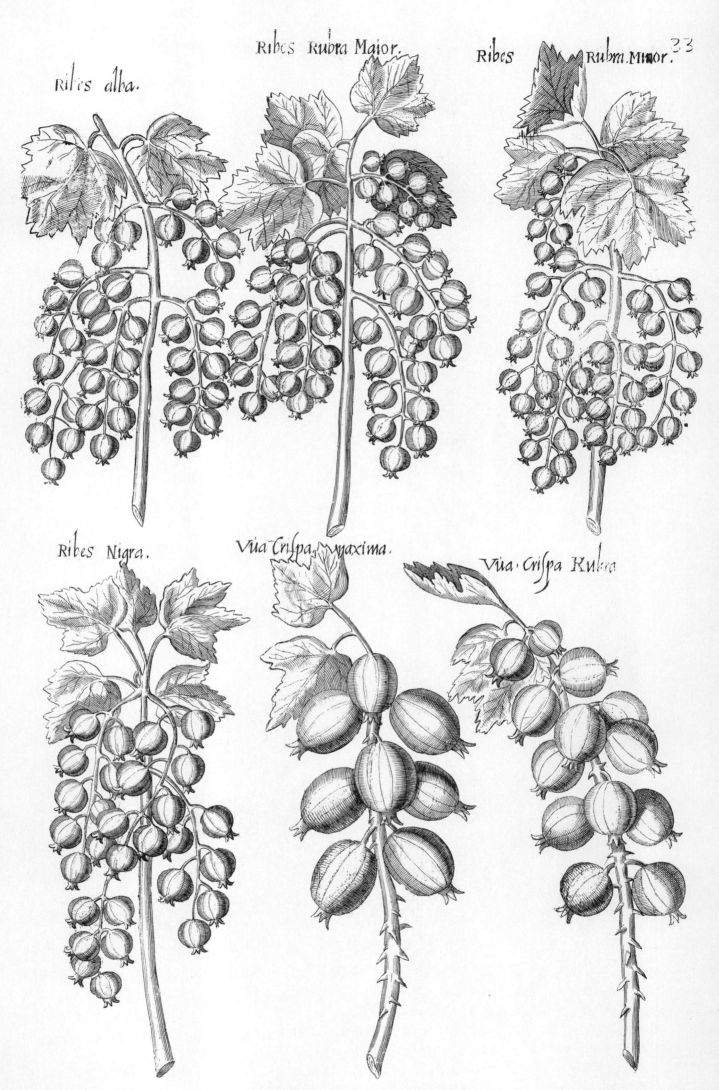

Ribes alba.

Ribes Rubra Maior.

Ribes Rubra Minor.

33

Ribes Nigra.

Vua Crispa maxima.

Vua Crispa Rubra

II-33 Currants and Gooseberries.

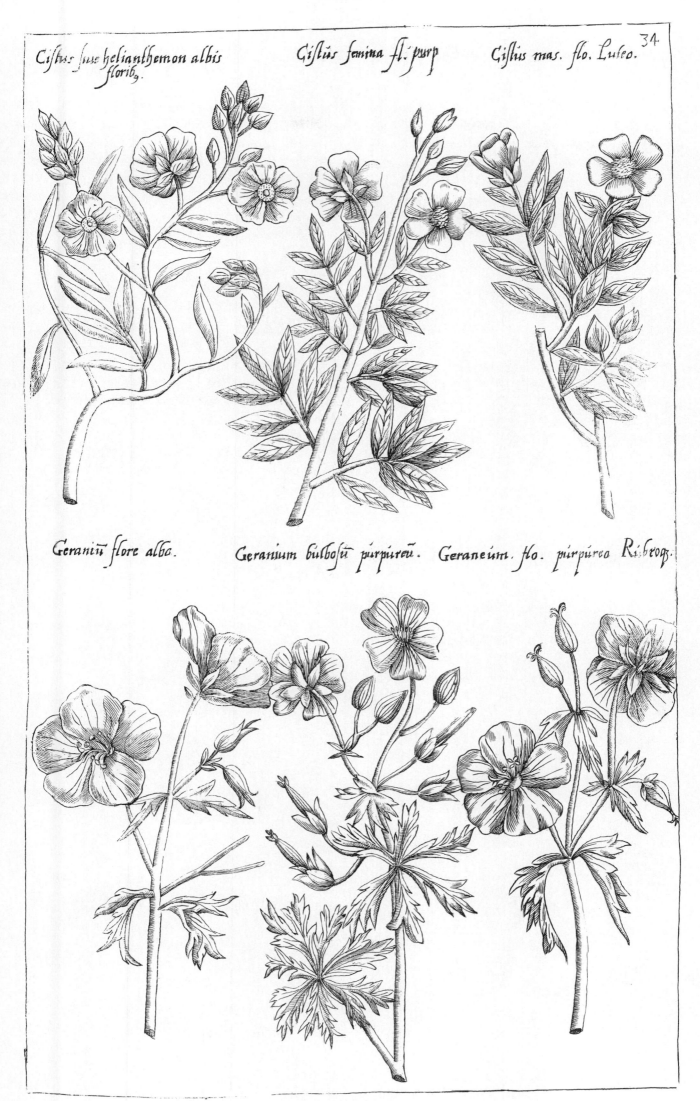

Cistus sue helianthemon albis florib₉.　　Cistus femina fl. purp　　Cistus mas. flo. Luteo.

Geraniū flore albo.　　Geranium bulbosū purpureū.　Geraneum. flo. purpureo Ribroz.

II-34　Various Plants.

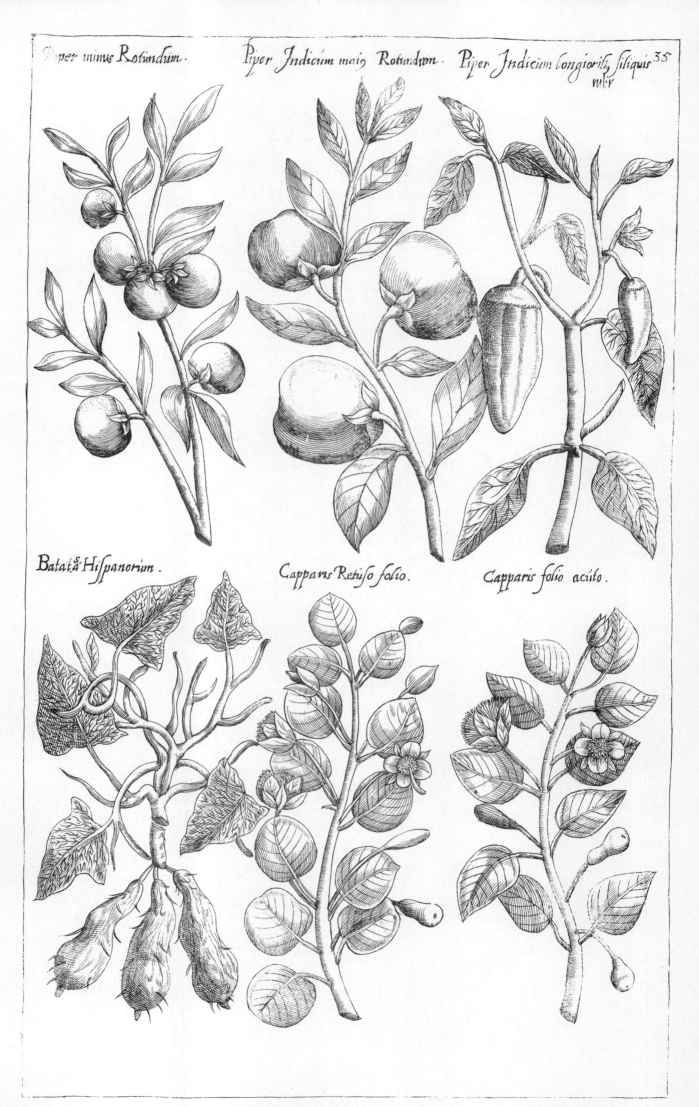

Piper minus Rotundum. Piper Indicum maig Rotundum. Piper Indicum longioriss, siliquis 35
rubr

Batatâ Hispanorum. Capparis Retiso folio. Capparis folio acuto.

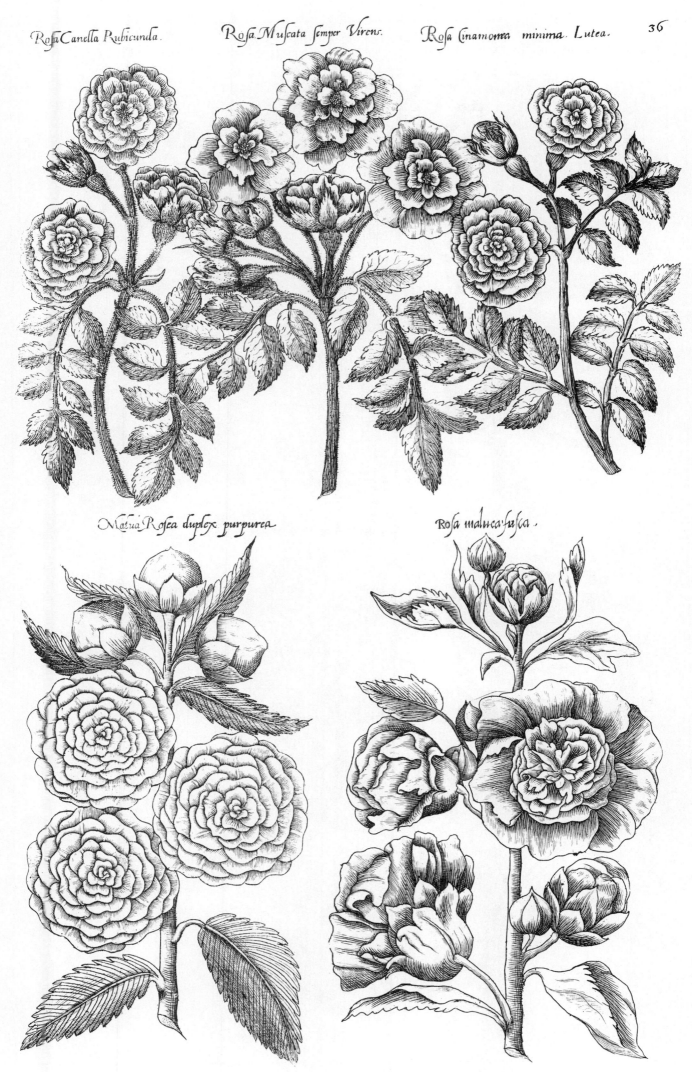

RosaCanella Rubicunda.   Rosa Muscata semper Virens.   Rosa Cinamonea minima Lutea.

Malua Rosea duplex purpurea   Rosa maluca fusca.

II-36   Roses and Other Plants.

Rosa Batauica maxima, siue Centifolia.

Rosa lutea Pleno flore.

Rosa   Alba   Rosa alba lineis suaue rubentibus prædita.

Rosa Damascena siue prouincialis

II-37   Roses.

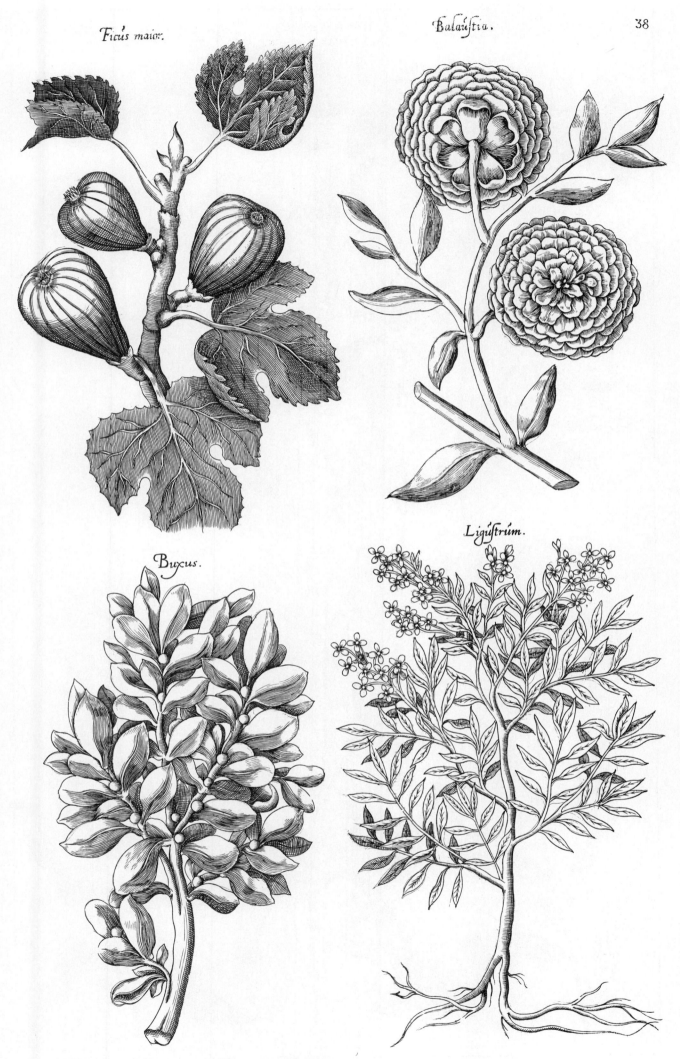

Ficus maior.

Balaustia.

38

Buxus.

Ligustrum.

II-38 Various Trees and Shrubs.

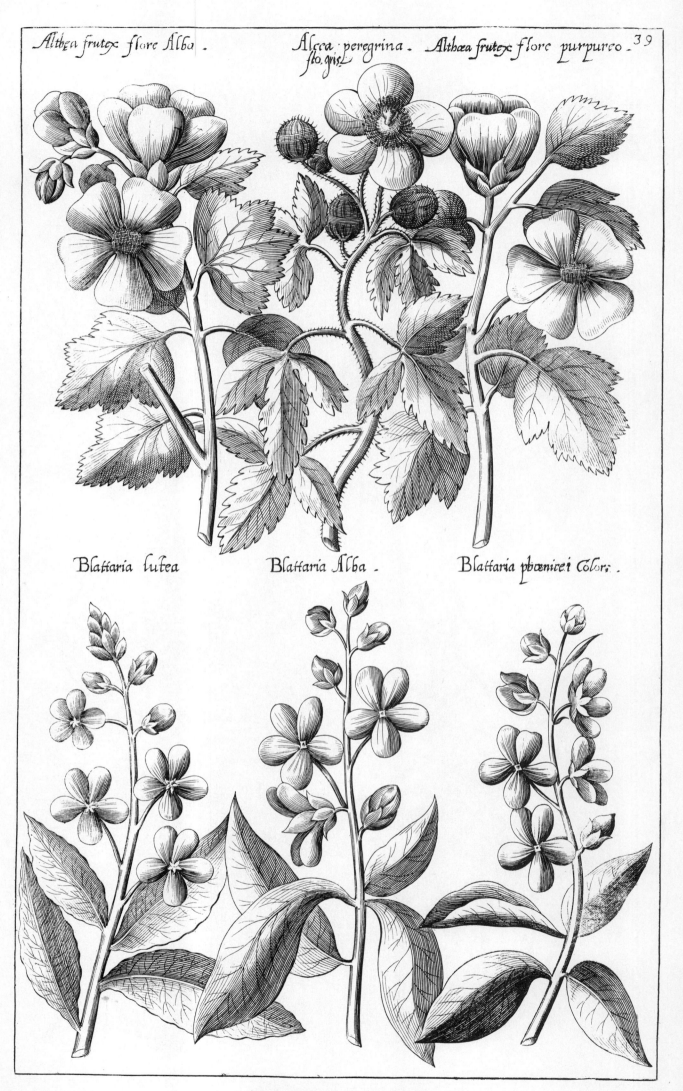

Althea frutex flore Alba . *Alcea peregrina .* *Althæa frutex flore purpureo .*
fto. gris.

Blattaria lutea *Blattaria Alba .* *Blattaria phœnicei Colori .*

II-39 Hibiscus and Mulleins.

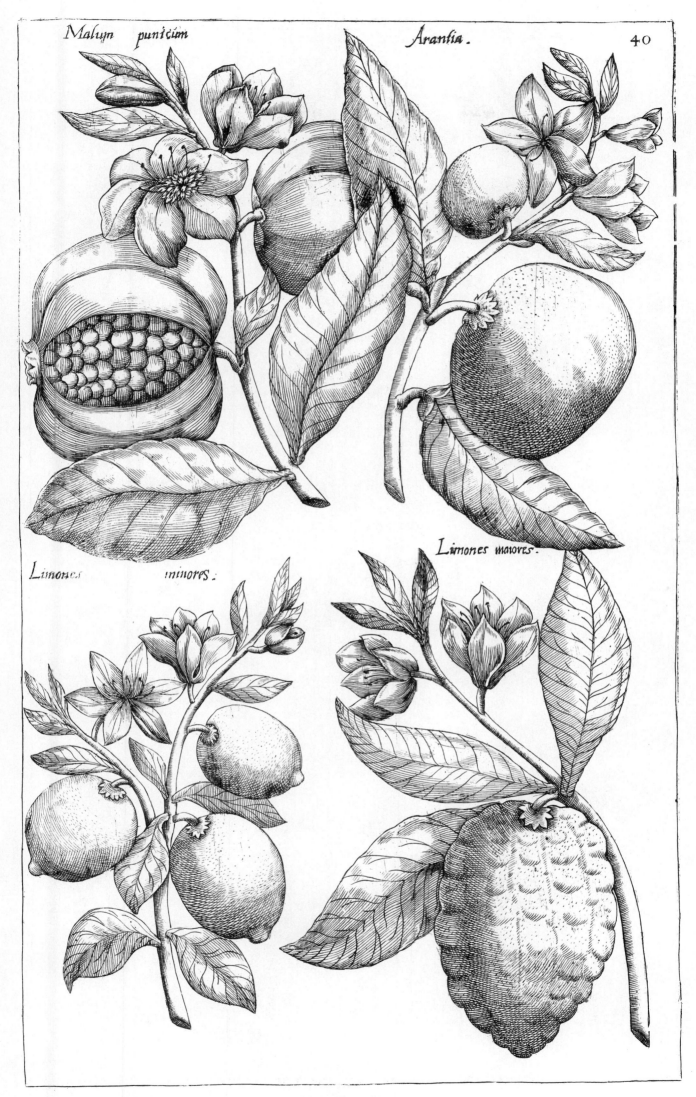

Malum punicum

Arantia.

Limones minores.

Limones maiores.

Laurus pusilla.   Nerion floribus albis.   Oleander Laurus Rosea. 4

Syringa Cærulea.   Syringa alba.   Laurus.

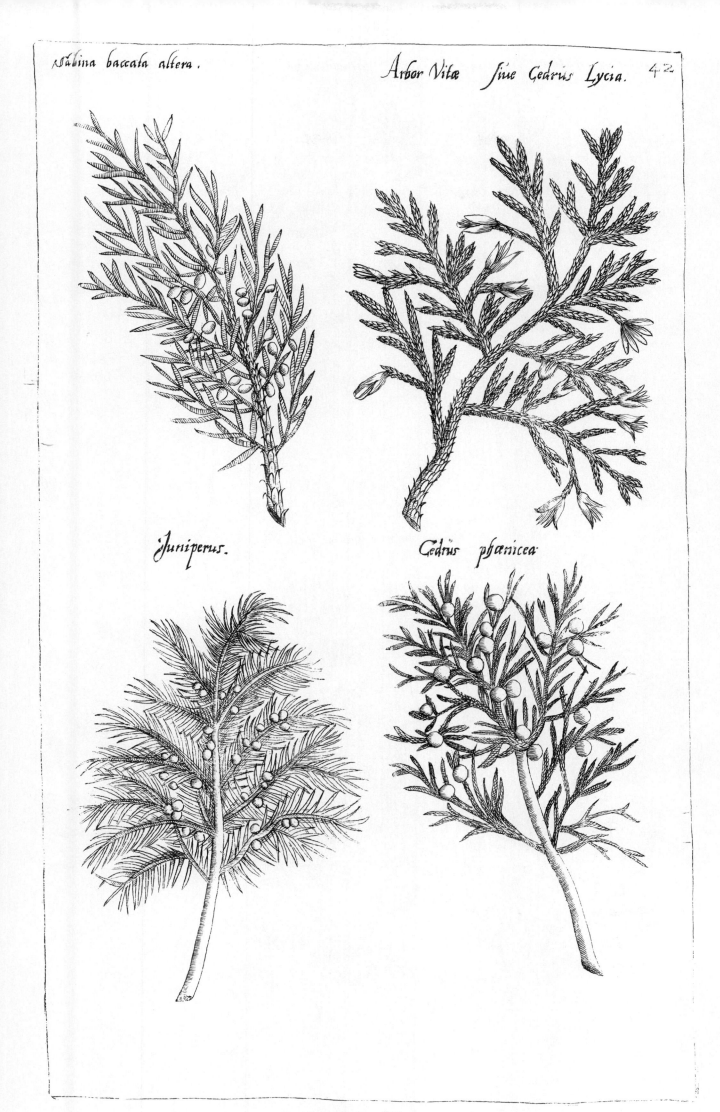

Juniperus.   Cedrus phœnicea

II-42 Junipers and Evergreens.

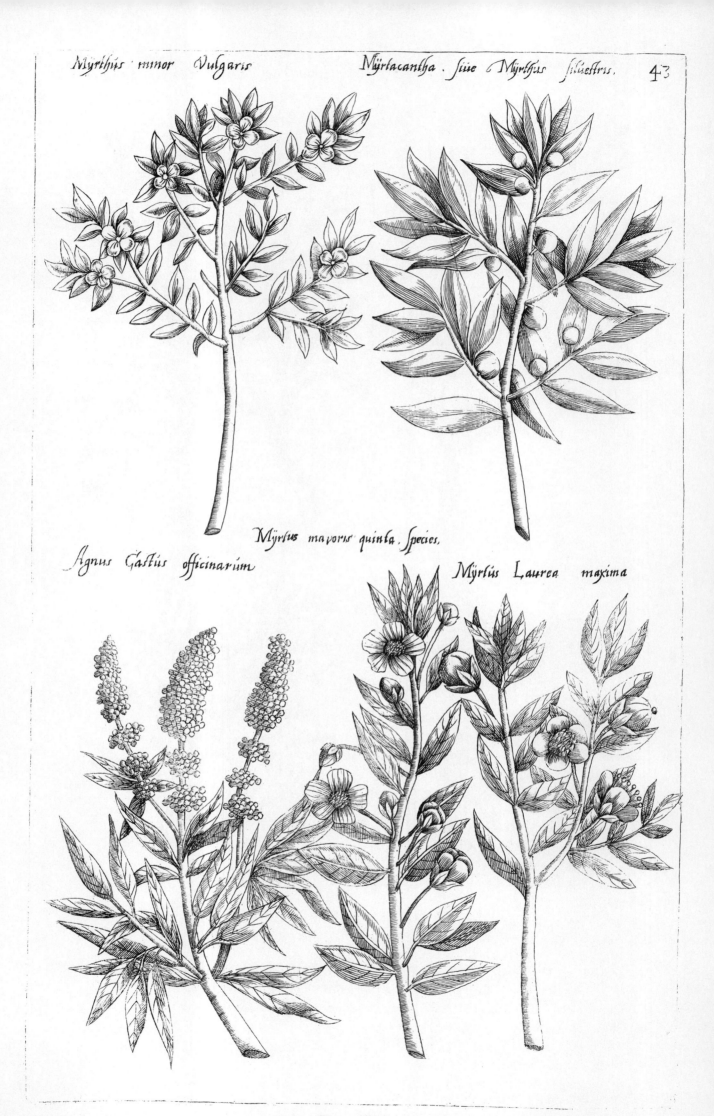

Myrthus minor Vulgaris

Myrtacantha. siue Myrthus siluestris.

Myrtus mayoris quinta. Species.

Agnus Castus officinarum

Myrtus Laurea maxima

DESCRIPTION
OF PLATES

1 *Fritillaria imperialis*. CROWN IMPERIAL. Left to right: Orange-red form. / Bulb. / Yellow, double-crowned, monstrous form.

2 Probably all garden forms of *Anemone coronaria*. WINDFLOWER. Left to right, top to bottom: Greenish white with violet stripes. / Double red. / Greenish white with red stripes. / Orange-red. / Tubers and foliage. / Vermilion, white ring at base. / Pink. / Reddish purple. / Orange. / Crimson. / Dark violet. / Flesh color. / Lavender. / Purple. / Tubers and Foliage.

3 Left column: Garden forms of *Anemone*. WINDFLOWER. Top to bottom: Dull white. / Lavender. / Grayish white. / Pink. / Blue. / Tuber. All with white center. Center column, top to bottom: *Anemone nemorosa*. Double form, pink and white. / *Eranthis hiemalis*. Yellow. / *Eranthis hiemalis*. Tuber. / *Anemone* sp. Blue. / *Anemone* sp. Violet. / *Anemone* sp. White. Right column, top to bottom: *Anemone hortensis*? White. / *Anemone palmata*? Yellow. / *Anemone palmata*? Yellow. / *Anemone sylvestris*. SNOWDROP. White. / *Anemone sylvestris*. SNOWDROP. White.

4 Probably all garden forms of *Anemone pavonina*. Left to right, top to bottom: Crimson. / Velvety red. / White outside, purple inside. / Dark red. / White, dark lines. / "Apple-blossom pink." / Dark red. / White. / Monstrous form. / White and grayish. / Double red, "Byzantine." / Double red, "Byzantine." / Plant.

5 Left column, top to bottom: *Crocus chrysanthus*? or other annelate species. White, brownish-purple veins. / *Crocus vernus*. Light bluish lavender. / *Crocus vernus*. White. Center column, top to bottom: *Crocus vernus*. White. / *Crocus aureus*. Yellow. Right column, top to bottom: *Crocus susianus*? *Romulea*? Yellow, purplish-brown stripes. / *Crocus reticulatus*? Bluish lilac, purplish-brown stripes. / *Crocus vernus*. Light lavender. Unnatural appearance is caused by omission of sheathing leaves.

6 Left column, top to bottom: *Crocus cancellatus*? Grayish blue. / *Crocus medius*? Pale lavender, dark center. / *Crocus clusius*? Purplish red. Center column, top to bottom: *Crocus speciosus*? Blue with violet lines. / *Crocus sativus*. SAFFRON CROCUS. Purple. / *Crocus longiflorus*? Bluish violet. Right column, top: *Erythronium dens canis*. DOG'S-TOOTH-VIOLET. Left: Pink. Right: White. Bottom: *Colchicum autumnale alboplenum*. DOUBLE-WHITE COLCHICUM. Sheaths are missing. The single leaf with some forms seems to indicate that leaves do not occur with the flowers. Speciation doubtful in most cases.

7 Top row, left to right: *Fritillaria lusitanica*. Purplish brown outside, yellowish green inside. / *Fritillaria obliqua*? Purplish brown. / *Fritillaria pyrenaica*. Unusual form, with more than one flower. Brownish. / *Fritillaria meleagris*. GUINEA-HEN FLOWER. Cream with red or purple checks. Bottom row, left: *Fritillaria meleagris*. GUINEA-HEN FLOWER. White form. Right: *Fritillaria lutea*? Yellow.

8 Top left: *Tulipa clusiana*. Reddish center, white edges. All others: Garden varieties of TULIP. Left to right, top to bottom: Tricolor; white, yellow, crimson flaming. / Deep pink with white edges; "not seen by me, but I have heard of it in writing from France." / White with lilac feathering. / White with crimson feathering. / White with reddish-purple spots and stripes. / Yellow with red feathering. / Bluish bottom, white middle, reddish top. / Pink. / Yellow and red; "called Cloth of Gold in Dutch." / Yellow and red. / White with black base.

9 Garden varieties of TULIP. Left to right, top to bottom: Red with yellow edges. / White with crimson flaming. / Yellow with red flaming. / Purple with white edges. / Crimson (or white? as in contents page). / White with crimson flaming. / Lavender with purple veins. / Yellow with red flaming. / Sulphur yellow with red edges. / Red with white ring, black base. / Yellow suffused with red. / Crimson with white edges.

10 TULIPS, garden varieties. Left to right, top to bottom: Light purple, white edges. / Yellow with red flaming; "called Laprock." / Pale lavender with purple stripes. / Sulphur yellow with red streaks. / White suffused with yellow, red streaks. / Yellow, edges sulphur yellow, red rings and spotting, base greenish yellow and black. / Purple. / Seed pod. / Seeds. / Bulb and leaves. / Purplish red, white edges.

11 Large bulbs: *Hyacinthus orientalis*. HYACINTH. Left to right: White. / Blue. / Pink. / Violet. Petals should not be separated. Small bulbs: *Hyacinthus amethystinus*? or a *Scilla*? Left: Blue. Right: White.

12 Sides: *Hyacinthus sp. orientalis*? Left: White. Right: Double, greenish. Center: *Hyacinthus orientalis*. HYACINTH. Garden forms. Blue, white, pink, purple, yellow available.

13 Left to right: *Endymion hispanicus*. SPANISH BLUEBELLS. Blue. / *Endymion hispanicus*. SPANISH BLUEBELLS. White. / *Muscari sp. comosus*? Purple. / *Dipcadi serotinum*. Greenish brown. / *Allium sp.*? Pink. The contents page mentions a white "Hyacinthus comosus" which was added to this plate in the later editions.

14 Left to right: *Polianthes tuberosa*. TUBEROSE. White. / Unidentified bulb. "Hyac. of Sweerts, from India, from Capo de Bona Speranza (Cape of Good Hope), bulb reddish white with many small pointed leaves." / *Polianthes gracilis*? Or a smaller variety of *P. tuberosa*? White.

15 Left to right, top to bottom: *Scilla bifolia*? White. / *Hyacinthus azureus*? Blue. / *Scilla bifolia*? Blue. / *Scilla bifolia*? Violet. / *Gagea sp.* Greenish yellow. / *Scilla bifolia*? Pink. / *Scilla autumnalis*. White form. / *Scilla monophyllos*. Blue.

16 *Scilla peruviana*. Left: Blue. Right: White.

17 Left to right: *Scilla hyacinthoides*? Blue. / *Scilla sp.* Blue. / *Scilla lilio-hyacinthus*. Blue. / *Scilla autumnalis*? Purplish-blue form.

18 Left: "Bloomed 1612, with many pale blue flowers like the Hyacinth of Peru [*Scilla peruvianus*], by Sweerts, not previously described." The German and Dutch contents pages state that this is from the West Indies; the French and Latin, from Africa. Possibly an early *Agapanthus*? Right: "From India, from the island, Capo de Bona Speranza; the bulb is large and whitish, the leaves a hand-breadth more or less, and coarsely splashed with purple. Described by Sweerts. Has not bloomed yet." Possibly *Haemanthus tigrina*?

19 Top row: *Muscari botyroides*. GRAPE HYACINTH. Left to right: Pink. / White. / Blue. Center row: *Muscari moschatum*? Left to right: Bluish purple. / Yellow. / Pink. Bottom row: Left: *Muscari moschatum*? White. Right: *Muscari sp.* Blue. Bulbs are all too large.

20 Left to right: *Leucoium vernum*. SNOWFLAKE. White. This may be intended as a representation of *Galanthus nivalis* (SNOWDROP), in which case the three outer petals should be longer than the three inner. / *Leucoium aestivum*? White. / *Leucoium pulchellum*. AUTUMN SNOWFLAKE. White. / *Leucoium trichophyllum*? White. / *Leucoium vernum vagneri*. GIANT SNOWFLAKE. White.

21 Top row (of blooms), left to right: *Narcissus pseudo-narcissus obvallaris*? Very badly drawn. Light yellow. / *Narcissus pseudo-narcissus major*. GREAT TRUMPET DAFFODIL. Golden yellow. / *Narcissus pseudo-narcissus*. DAFFODIL, smaller form. Golden yellow. Center row (of blooms), left to right: *Narcissus abscissus*. White perianth, yellow trumpet. / *Narcissus sp.* Pale yellow. *N. parviflorus*? / *Narcissus pseudo-narcissus*. Double form, yellow. Bottom row (of blooms), left to right: *Narcissus alpestris*. White. / *Narcissus bulbocodium*. Yellow. / *Narcissus minor*. Yellow.

22 Left to right: *Narcissus elegans*. Yellow or white, autumn-flowering. / *Narcissus poeticus*. White with orange-red cup. / *Narcissus tazetta*. Yellow. / *Narcissus dubius*? or *N. tazetta*? White with red cup.

23 *Narcissus tazetta*. Left to right: Italian form, white with yellow cup. / Yellow. / White with yellow cup.

24 Probably all forms of *Narcissus tazetta*. Left to right: White, double cup. / Light yellow. / White, yellow cup, "from Pisa, with many white flowers." / Light yellow. / White (*Narcissus papyreus*). (Contents page followed for colors.)

25 Forms of *Narcissus incomparabilis*. All bicolors, with white perianth, trumpet in shades of yellow.

26 Left to right: *Narcissus tazetta*. Double form, white. / *Narcissus incomparabilis*. Double, monstrous form. White, "closely filled with four or five yellow calixes." / *Narcissus poeticus*. Double form, yellow. / *Narcissus poeticus*. Double form, yellow. / *Narcissus poeticus*. Double form, white.

27 Left: *Pancratium illyricum*. White. "Narc. of Matthioli. I have had this with 27 flowers on a stalk." Right: *Pancratium maritimum*? White. Poorly drawn.

28 Left to right: *Zephyranthes atamasco*? Pink. "Narcissus of Virginia of Pet. Garet." / *Sprekelia formosissima*. Red. "Narcissus from India per Jacobeus, leaves like an autumn crocus." / *Sternbergia Fischeriana* or *S. macrantha*. Yellow. "Like autumn crocus, but blossoms in spring."

29 Left to right: *Narcissus triandrus albus*. White. / *Narcissus Jonquilla*. Variant. Yellow with white streaks on petals. / *Narcissus Jonquilla*. Double yellow. / *Narcissus* sp. JONQUIL group or hybrid. Yellow. "Flowers long after the others are past; not before described." / *Narcissus* sp. JONQUIL group or hybrid. Yellow. / *Narcissus* sp. JONQUIL group or hybrid. Yellow.

30 Top row, left to right: *Narcissus junctifolius*. Taken from L'Obel; either inaccurate or a lost form. / *Narcissus viridiflorus*? AUTUMN-FLOWERING DAFFODIL. Greenish white. / *Narcissus bulbocodium*. Yellow. Bottom row, left: *Narcissus serotinus*. Traditional, highly inaccurate representation. Center & right: Possibly bad renderings of PANCRATIUMS, reduced in size. "With purple, red, white and yellow flowers; has not bloomed with us."

31 Unidentified. "Have not flowered with us yet; not previously described." Left: "From East Indies." Right: "From West Indies."

32 Unidentified. "Have not flowered with us yet; not previously described." Left: "From East Indies." Right: "From West Indies."

33 Left to right: "Narc. or Pancratium of Clusius; has not flowered yet." / *Urginea maritima*. SEA SQUILL. White. / "Smaller Sea Squill from Spain." / "Narc. or Pancratium; not brought to this country yet."

34 Garden varieties of *Iris xiphioides*. ENGLISH IRIS. Top left: White, with violet-blue stripes. Top right: White. Bottom left: Blue with heavy violet lines, or white with violet. Bottom right: Purple.

35 Top row, left to right: *Iris xiphium*. SPANISH IRIS. White. / Possibly very early appearance of *Iris reticulata*? From Persia. Purple. / *Iris xiphium*. SPANISH IRIS. Yellow. Bottom row, left to right: *Iris xiphium*. SPANISH IRIS. Purple. / *Iris, Juno* subgenus. Bluish. / *Iris xiphium*. SPANISH IRIS. Blue.

36 Left to right: *Iris Xiphium* subgenus. Purplish blue. / *Iris, Juno* subgenus. *I. alata*? Purple. / *Hermodactylus tuberosus*. Falls purple, standards greenish.

37 Top row: *Iris spuria*. Left to right: Double blue. / White. / Blue. Bottom: *Iris siberica*? SIBERIAN IRIS. White or purple.

38 Left: *Iris sambucina* or *squalens*. Purple. Right: *Iris susiana*. Dull white with purplish-brown markings.

39 Left: *Iris, oncocyclus* subgenus. Like *I. susiana*, but smaller. *Iris lorteti*? but falls should not be divided. Right: *Iris oncocyclus* subgenus.

40 Top left: *Iris pallida*. Blue. Inflorescence badly drawn. Top right: *Iris pumila*. White. Bottom row, left to right: *Iris cengialti*. Blue falls, light purple standards. White form of this is sometimes called *Iris swerti*, after Sweerts. / *Iris variegata*. Yellow with brown markings. / *Iris pumila*. Purple.

41 Extremities: *Iris, pogoniris* subgenus, tall varieties. Top left: White and blue. Top right:

Yellow. "From Tripoli." Bottom left: Purple (*Iris albicans?*). Bottom right: Violet. Center: *Iris pumila*. Dark purple.

42 Left to right: *Gladiolus communis*. Pink. / *Gladiolus byzantinus?* Dark purple. / *Gladiolus* sp. Lavender. / *Gladiolus communis*. White.

43 Left to right: *Arum italicum*. / *Arum tenuifolium?* / *Dracunculus vulgaris*. Foliage, flower and tuber.

44 Left: *Fritillaria persica*. Purple. Right: *Fritillaria latifolia?* Multiple-flowered variety. Badly drawn.

45 Left: *Lilium candidum*. MADONNA LILY. White. Right: Historically, probably a white martagon lily, but the illustration does not fit well.

46 Left to right: *Lilium aurantiacum*. Yellowish. / *Lilium aurantiacum*. Orange with black spots. / *Lilium bulbiferum*. Red. Bulbils should be in the axils of the leaves.

47 Left to right: *Hemerocallis fulva*. DAYLILY. Orange red. Poorly drawn. / *Hemerocallis flava*. YELLOW DAYLILY. Yellow. Poorly drawn. / *Anthericum liliago?* ST. JOHN'S LILY. White.

48 Left to right: *Anthericum ramosum?* or, less likely, *Asphodelus ramosus?* White. Stylized representation. / *Asphodeline lutea*. ASPHODEL. Yellow. / *Asphodelus ramosus*. White.

49 Left: *Lilium pomponium*. SCARLET TURKSCAP LILY. Coral red. / Right: *Lilium chalcedonicum?* Red.

50 Forms of *Lilium chalcedonicum?* Red. "From Constantinople."

51 Left: *Lilium monadelphum?* Yellow. "With 70 or 80 blossoms on one stalk. Not previously described." Right: *Lilium pyrenaicum?* Greenish yellow.

52 Forms of *Lilium martagon*. MARTAGON LILY. Left: White, unspotted. Right: Grayish with spots.

53 Forms of *Lilium martagon*. MARTAGON LILY. Purple, white, pinkish, lilac. Foliage should be whorled.

54 Top row, left to right: *Ranunculus asiaticus*. Double form, white inside, red outside. / *Ranunculus bullatus*. Yellow. / *Ranunculus asiaticus*. Double form, orange vermilion. Bottom row, left to right: *Ranunculus asiaticus*. Brownish red. "From Tripoli, short roots." / *Ranunculus bulbosus, flore pleno*. Yellow, cultivated variety. / *Ranunculus asiaticus*. White sprinkled with pink.

55 Top row, left to right: *Caltha palustris*. MARSH MARIGOLD. Yellow, double form. / *Ranunculus asiaticus*. Yellow with red stripes. / *Ranunculus aconitifolius*. Double white form. Roots should be more tuberous. Bottom left: *Ranunculus repens?* BUTTERCUP. Double form, yellow. Bottom right: *Trollius europeus*. GLOBEFLOWER. Yellow.

56 Top row, left to right: *Bulbocodium vernum*. Purple. / *Colchicum autumnale*. White, striped with purple. / *Colchicum* sp., tessellated group. *C. varietatum?* Reddish and white. Bottom row, left to right: *Sternbergia lutea*. Yellow. / *Colchicum autumnale*. White and pink double variety. / *Colchicum autumnale*. Pale pink. Leaves are not present at the same time as the flowers in the Colchicums.

57 Left to right: *Ornithogalum arabicum*. White with black ovary in center. / *Ornithogalum umbellatum*. Not on same scale as other plants on plate. / *Ornithogalum nutans*. Inside white, outside grayish green. / *Gagea foliosa?* Yellow.

58 Left to right: *Ornithogalum narbonense?* Or *O. pyrenaicum?* White, with green stripes. / *Ornithogalum unifolium*. White. / *Fritillaria libanotica?* White. Bulb too large.

59 Bottom left: *Cyclamen orbiculatum coum*. White. All others: *Cyclamen neapolitanum*. Pink. Marbled leaves.

60 Left to right: *Allium* sp. Purple. Unusual *A. scorodoprasum?* / *Allium clusianum?* White. / *Allium moly*. Yellow. / *Allium triquetrum pendulinum*. White, striped with green. / *Allium roseum?* Pink.

61 Left to right: *Allium paniculatum*. Or *A. kermesinum?* Reddish violet. / *Allium* sp. perhaps Central Asiatic origin? / *Allium ursinum*. RAMSON, WILD GARLIC. White.

62 Left, center: *Gynandriris sisyrinchium*. Blue, yellow markings. Right: *Haemanthus multiflorus?* BLOOD-FLOWER. "From Guinea."

63 Top row, left to right: *Ophrys apifera*. BEE ORCHID. Pinkish. / *Orchis mascula?* Purple and brown. / *Orchis purpurea?* Light purple, lighter spots. / *Ophrys bertholonii?* Purple. / *Anacamptis pyramidalis?* Purplish red. Bottom row, left to right: *Orchis* sp. Purplish red. / *Orchis latifolia?* Red. / *Orchis maculata?* Purple to white. / *Orchis incarnata?* White, reddish spots. Speciation very uncertain.

64 Garden varieties of *Paeonia officinalis*. Top left: Double red. Top right: Double pink, fading to white. Bottom: Single white.

65 Top row, left to right: *Hyacinthus romanus?* ROMAN HYACINTH. White. / "Hyacinth with leafy stalk." Apparently a monstrous form of *Hyacinthus orientalis*, recorded by Clusius. / Questionable as *Zinziber* (GINGER). Probably an *Iris* sp. Bottom row, left to right: *Narcissus* sp. Double white form with spike in center. Claimed to come from Virginia. / *Narcissus juncifolius*. RUSH-LEAF JONQUIL. Yellow. / *Narcissus minor*, white form? / *Colchicum cilicium?* Purple.

66 Left: *Gladiolus* sp. Scarlet and pink. Top right: *Crassula* sp? Not a bulb, but a succulent. Bottom right: *Pachypodium* sp.? Not a bulb, but a succulent.

67 Unidentified bulbs from South Africa. Amaryllids?

II-1 Top left: *Helleborus viridis?* Greenish white. Top right: *Helleborus niger*. CHRISTMAS ROSE. White. Leaves should be smooth, thick, glossy. Bottom left: *Cypripedium calceolus*. LADY'S SLIPPER. Yellow and brown tones. Bottom right: *Adonis vernalis*. SPRING ADONIS. Yellow.

II-2 Left to right, top and center rows: *Viola odorata?* White. / *Viola tricolor*, or similar garden pansy. Yellow. / *Viola tricolor*, or similar garden pansy. Violet. / *Viola odorata*. Blue. / *Viola odorata*. Double form, blue. / *Viola* sp. Purple. Bottom row: *Fragaria*. Garden varieties of STRAWBERRY. Left to right: White-fruited. / Large-fruited. / Small-fruited.

II-3 Top and center rows: *Hepatica nobilis*. Garden forms. Left to right: White. / Double blue. / Pale lavender. / Blue. / Red. / Violet. Also called *Anemone hepatica*. Bottom row: *Bellis perennis*. ENGLISH DAISY. Garden forms. Left to right: Red. / Variegated pink and white. / White.

II-4 Top row: *Primula auricula*. AURICULA. Garden forms. Left to right: Brownish. / Pink. / White. Center row, left to right: *Ramondia pyrenaica*. Blue. / *Primula auricula*. AURICULA. Garden form. Yellow. / *Primula auricula*. AURICULA. Garden form. Red. Bottom row, left to right: *Primula polyantha*. PRIMROSE. Double form, yellow. / *Primula auricula*. AURICULA. Garden form. Purple. / *Primula veris*. COWSLIP. Purple form.

II-5 Garden varieties of *Mathiola incana*. STOCK. Top row, left to right: Double purple, green lines. / Double purple, variegated. / Double violet. Bottom row, left to right: Purplish red. / Yellow. / White. All not well drawn.

II-6 Top left: *Digitalis purpurea*. FOXGLOVE. White. Top right: *Digitalis Thapsi?* Purple. Bottom left: *Digitalis oscura*. Yellow. Bottom right: *Digitalis ferruginea*. Brownish yellow. All stylized.

II-7 Top row, left to right: *Polygonatum multiflorum*. SOLOMON'S SEAL. White. / *Convallaria majalis*. LILY OF THE VALLEY. Pink. / *Convallaria majalis*. LILY OF THE VALLEY. White. Bottom row, left to right: *Corydalis cava*. HOLLOW ROOT. White. / *Corydalis fabacea?* Deep pink. / *Corydalis Halleri?* Purple.

II-8 Garden forms of *Aquilegia vulgaris*. COLUMBINE. Left to right, top to bottom: Double white. / Double red. / Double, mixed colors. / Double, reddish brown. / Blue spurs, white center. / Pink. / Star-formed pink. / Star-formed violet. / Blue.

II-9 Probably all garden forms of *Delphinium ajacis*. ROCKET LARKSPUR. Top left: Double white. Top right: Variegated. Bottom left: Blue. Bottom right: Pink.

II-10 Top row, left to right: *Aconitum napellus*. MONKSHOOD. Blue. / *Aconitum* sp. Blue. / *Aconitum anthora aureum*. Yellow. Center row: *Centaurea cyanus*. BACHELOR'S BUTTONS. Left to right: White. / Double pink. / Double purple. Bottom row, left to right: *Lychnis chalcedonica*. MALTESE CROSS. Pink. / *Lychnis chalcedonica*. MALTESE CROSS. Orange red. / *Centaurea cyanus*. BACHELOR'S BUTTONS. Blue.

II-11 Top row, left: *Anemone pulsatilla*, PASQUE FLOWER. White form. Top row, right: *Anemone pratensis*. Dark purple. Center row: *Lychnis* sp. CAMPION. Left to right: Double red. / Double white. / Red. / White and red. Bottom row: *Calendula officinalis*. Orange or yellow.

II-12 Top left: *Clematis viticella*. Purplish red or blue. Top right: *Clematis* sp. Double form, bluish purple. Perhaps *C. viticella*. Bottom left: *Lonicera periclymenum?* HONEYSUCKLE, WOODBINE. Yellow, red inside. Bottom right: *Vinca major*. GREAT PERIWINKLE. Blue.

II-13 Top row, left to right: *Chrysanthemum parthenium*. FEVERFEW. Double white form. / *Anacyclus valentinus*. Badly drawn. / *Cortusa matthioli*. Blue. Bottom row, left to right: *Adonis aestivalis*. Orange. / *Adonis annua?* Red. / *Gnaphalium* sp.? CUDWEED.

II-14 Left to right, top to bottom: *Gentiana pneumonanthe?* Blue. / *Gentiana vulgaris?* Blue. / *Gentiana vulgaris?* Blue. / *Ipomoea purpurea?* Blue form. / *Gentiana* sp.? *Campanula* sp.? Blue. / *Gentiana* sp.? *Campanula* sp.? Blue. / *Convolvulus* sp. *C. scammonia?* Red. / *Convolvulus* sp. *C. scammonia?* White. / *Ipomoea nil*. Blue. Top row illustrations should have five lobes on the flowers. In de Bry's use of these plates, this has been corrected.

II-15 Top left: *Nigella damascena*. LOVE-IN-A-MIST. Blue. Top right: *Nigella sativa*. Blue. Bottom: *Nigella hispanica*. Blue.

II-16 Top row, left to right: *Campanula persicifolia*. WILLOW BELLS. White. / *Campanula pyramidalis*. PYRAMID BELLFLOWER. Blue. / *Campanula persicifolia*. WILLOW BELLS. Blue. Bottom row, left to right: *Campanula* sp. *C. trachelium?* White. / *Campanula* sp. *C. trachelium?* Blue. / *Campanula medium?* CANTERBURY BELLS. Purple form. Leaves should be more serrated.

II-17 Garden forms of *Dianthus caryophilus*. CARNATION. Left to right, top to bottom: White, feathered and spotted with red. / White, striped with red. / White, striped with red. / White. / Pink. / Red with darker red spots. / Greenish white. / Red. / White with crimson stripes, smaller form.

II-18 Left to right, top to bottom: *Dianthus superbus*. White with red markings. / *Dianthus plumarius*. Double white. / *Dianthus plumarius*. Double red. / *Dianthus barbatus*. SWEET JOHN. White with red zones. / *Dianthus barbatus*. SWEET JOHN. Pink or red. / *Dianthus caryophilus?* Double variety. White or pink or red. / *Dianthus plumarius?* Single. Possibly other species. / *Dianthus barbatus*. SWEET WILLIAM. Red. / *Dianthus barbatus*. SWEET WILLIAM. White.

II-19 Top row: *Dictamnus albus*. GASPLANT. Left: White. Right: White and blue. Bottom row: *Antirrhinum majus*. SNAPDRAGON. Left: White. Right: Red.

II-20 Top left: *Solanum melongena*. EGGPLANT. Top right: *Lycopersicum esculentum*. TOMATO. Bottom left: *Atropa belladonna*. BELLADONNA. Bottom right: *Physalis alkekengi*. HUSK CHERRY.

II-21 Left to right, top to bottom: *Amaranthus caudatus*. Red. / *Celosia argentea*. COXCOMB. Yellow. / *Celosia argentea*. COXCOMB. Red. / *Hedysarum* sp. *H. coronarium?* FRENCH HONEYSUCKLE. Red. / *Amaranthus tricolor?* JOSEPH'S COAT. Flowers exaggerated. / *Amaranthus paniculatus*. Red. / *Phaca boetica*. BASTARD VETCH. Red. Or *Astragalus?* / *Trifolium incarnatum*. CRIMSON CLOVER. Crimson. / *Trifolium rubens?* HAREFOOT CLOVER. Red.

II-22 Top row: *Papaver somniferum*. OPIUM POPPY. Garden varieties. Left: Double pink. Right: Double white. Center row, left: *Glaucium corniculatum*. HORNED POPPY. Red. Center row, right: "From West Indies by Sweerts; also described by Clusius." Sweerts calls this a capsule from an "Indian Poppy." It looks more like a *Nelumbium* (LOTUS). Bottom row, left: *Papaver somniferum*. OPIUM POPPY. Garden variety. Double red. Bottom row, right: *Viburnum opulus*. GUELDER ROSE. White.

II-23 Top left: *Hesperis matronalis?* SWEET ROCKET. Purple or pink. Top right: *Dentaria pinnata*. Purple. Bottom row: *Nicotiana tabacum*. TOBACCO. Left: Large-leafed lavender-flowered. Right: Small-leafed purple-flowered.

II-24 Top row: *Mirabilis jalapa*. FOUR-O'CLOCK. Left: White and yellow. Right: Red and white.

Bottom left: *Jasminum* sp. If *J. officinale*, as is most probable, the leaves should be opposite. COMMON JASMINE. White. Bottom right: *Jasminum humile*. ITALIAN JASMINE. Yellow.

II-25 *Helianthus* sp. SUNFLOWER. Yellow with red inner ring, or yellow.

II-26 Top row: *Tagetes erecta*. AFRICAN MARIGOLD. Left: Double orange. Right: Single yellow. Bottom row: *Tagetes patula*. FRENCH MARIGOLD. Reddish browns and yellows.

II-27 Top left: *Vinis vinifera*. GRAPE. Top right: *Momordica balsamina*. BALSAM APPLE. Bottom left: *Rosmarinus officinalis*. ROSEMARY. Bottom right: Unidentified plant. The name Halicacabus (see engraved legend) was applied to plants with vesicular (bladder-like, air-filled) fruit, like a *Physalis*. This illustration, which appears in other early botanies, with no further significant information, is perhaps a member of the Solanaceae from America.

II-28 Top left: *Tropaeolum minor*. NASTURTIUM. Yellow with red stripes. Flower poorly drawn; de Bry's original better. Top right: *Tropaeolum* sp. Possibly a very badly stylized *T. peregrinum*? Bottom left: *Polemonium caeruleum*. GREEK VALERIAN. Blue. Bottom right: *Solanum tuberosum*. POTATO. Fruit and flowers too large.

II-29 Left to right, top to bottom: *Acanthus spinosus*. PRICKLY ACANTHUS. Purple or white. / *Acanthus mollis*. Acanthus of architecture. Purple or white. / *Carthamus tinctorius*? SAFFLOWER. Orange. / *Scorzonera hispanica*. BLACK SALSIFY. Yellow. / A composite, possibly *Inula* sp. or *Scorzonera* sp. Orange yellow. Although Sweerts calls this "atticus," Clusius describes it as from Spain. / *Aster amellus*. ITALIAN ASTER. Blue.

II-30 Top left: *Cactus melocactus*. Top right: *Opuntia ficus-indica*. INDIAN FIG, PRICKLY PEAR. Red. Bottom left: *Euphorbia* sp. *polygona*? Bottom right: Cactus of the Cereid group.

II-31 Top left: *Ananas comosus*. PINEAPPLE. "Made exactly from life, and cast; Schwertz owes this illustration to me," German contents page. Top right: *Tigridia pavonia*. White, spotted with red. Picture reduced and greatly stylized. "Described by Lobel; not hitherto known." Bottom left: *Agave americana*. AMERICAN ALOE. Yellow. Bottom right: *Aloe vera*? ALOES.

II-32 *Canna indica*. Left: Yellow form. Right: Red form.

II-33 Top row: *Ribes*. Garden varieties of CURRANT. Left to right: White. / Large red. / Small red. Bottom row, left to right: *Ribes*. Garden variety of CURRANT. Black. / *Ribes*. Garden variety of GOOSEBERRY. White. / *Ribes*. Garden variety of GOOSEBERRY. Red.

II-34 Top row: *Cistus* or *Helianthemum* sp. ROCK ROSE. Left to right: White. / Purple. / Yellow. Bottom row, left to right: *Geranium* sp. White. / *Geranium tuberosum*. Pink or purple. / *Geranium* sp. Purple.

II-35 Top row: *Capsicum frutescens*. PEPPERS, garden varieties. Left to right: Small cherry. / Bell. / Long red. Bottom row, left to right: *Ipomoea batatas*. SWEET POTATO. "From Spain, very good to eat." / *Capparis spinosa*. CAPER. / *Capparis ovata*. CAPER.

II-36 Top row, left to right: *Rosa cinnamomea*? CINNAMON ROSE. Double form, pink or red. / *Rosa moschata*. MUSK ROSE. Double form, white. / *Rosa hemispherica*? PERSIAN ROSE. Double form, yellow. Should be more spiny. Bottom row, left: Problematic. This plate greatly resembles *Hibiscus rosa-sinensis*, which was not introduced until much later. In de Bry's reuse of this illustration, it was redrawn to conform to a Hollyhock. Bottom row, right: *Althaea rosa*. HOLLYHOCK. Double form, purple.

II-37 Top left: *Rosa centifolia*. CABBAGE ROSE, BATAVIAN ROSE. Double. Red or white or pink. Top right: *Rosa foetida*. AUSTRIAN BRIAR ROSE. Double yellow. Bottom row, left to right: *Rosa alba*. Double white ROSE. / *Rosa gallica versicolor*. Red and white-striped double form. / *Rosa damascena*. DAMASK ROSE. Double pink. Thorns have been omitted.

II-38 Top left: *Ficus carica*. FIG. Top right: *Punica granatum nana*. WILD POMEGRANATE. Double red flowers. Bottom left: *Buxus sempervirens*. BOX. Bottom right: *Ligustrum vulgare*. PRIVET.

II-39 Left to right, top to bottom: *Hibiscus syriacus*. ROSE OF SHARON. Single white form. / *Hibiscus trionum*. FLOWER OF AN HOUR. Lavender. Globes represent inflated calyx. /

Hibiscus syriacus. ROSE OF SHARON. Single purple form. / *Verbascum blattaria?* Leaves probably incorrect. Yellow. / *Verbascum blattaria?* Leaves probably incorrect. White. / *Verbascum phoenicum*. Purple. All Verbascums badly drawn.

II-40 Top left: *Punica granatum*. POMEGRANATE. Top right: *Citrus* sp. ORANGE. Probably *C. sinensis*. SWEET ORANGE. Bottom left: *Citrus Limonia*. LEMON. Bottom right: *Citrus medica*. CITRON.

II-41 Left to right, top to bottom: *Daphne laureola?* SPURGE LAUREL. / *Nerium oleander*. OLEANDER. White. / *Nerium oleander*. OLEANDER. Pink. / *Laurus nobilis*. LAUREL. / *Syringa vulgaris*. LILAC. White. / *Syringa vulgaris*. LILAC. Blue. Note that the engraved captions are reversed for bottom row, left, and bottom row, right.

II-42 Top left: *Juniperus sabina?* SAVIN JUNIPER. Top right: *Cupressus* sp. Bottom left: *Juniperus communis*. JUNIPER. Bottom right: *Juniperus phoenicea*. All are so stylized that identification is questionable.

II-43 Top left: *Myrtus communis*. MYRTLE, garden variety. BOX MYRTLE. Top right: *Ruscus aculeatus*. BUTCHER'S BROOM. Bottom left: *Vitex agnus-casti*. CHASTE TREE. Bottom center and right: *Myrtus communis*. MYRTLE, garden varieties.